How To Buy A
$\mathcal{D}$IAMOND

FRED CUELLAR

SOURCEBOOKS, INC.

Naperville, Illinois

Published by: Sourcebooks, Inc.
P.O. Box 372, Naperville, Illinois 60566
(630) 961-3900
FAX: 630-961-2168

This publication is designed to provide accurate and authoritative information in regard to the subject matter covered. It is sold with the understanding that the publisher is not engaged in rendering legal, accounting, or other professional service. If legal advice or other expert assistance is required, the services of a competent professional person should be sought.
From a Declaration of Principles Jointly Adopted by a Committee of the American Bar Association and a Committee of Publishers and Associations

Diamond Information Line: 713-22-CARAT
Internet Web site: http://www.diamondcttersintl.com

Photograph of Fred Cuellar by Gittings Lorfing
Cover and inside photography by Leeming Studios • 401-941-9459
Media Relations & Marketing: LaTeace Towns-Cuellar

Library of Congress Cataloging-in-Publication Data

Cuellar, Fred.
    How to buy a diamond / Fred Cuellar.
            p. cm
        Includes index.
        ISBN 1-883518-11-3 (pbk.)
        1. Diamonds – Purchasing. 2. Rings – Purchasing. I. Title
    TS753.C83   1996   96-35321
    735'.23--dc20   CIP

                Printed and bound in the United States of America.
                    Paperback — 10 9 8 7 6 5 4 3 2 1

Dedication

This book is dedicated first to my mother and father.
This book would not have been possible without
their love and support.

Second, I dedicate this book to every man in love and
doing his best to make the love of his life happy by
buying the perfect diamond.

Third, and most of all, I dedicate this book to the
love of my life, LaTeace. She makes life worth living and I could
not imagine a better companion with whom to spend
all the days of my life.

Acknowledgements

LaTeace

Hector & Elvira

Greg J.P. Godek

Alfonso & Delia Cuellar

Jovita C. Montalvo &
the late Alfredo Montalvo

George & Betty Woody

Lisa and Knox Wright

Sha Shane, Cytinya,
& Junior

Rick & Kerry Antona

Chaim Shimonov

Neil Malhotra

Barry Berg

Emil Jay Greenberg

Miriam Rosen

Fawn Ross

Bill McNamara

Jim Speros

Montreal Allouettes

Houston Astros

Neil Talmedge

Steve Patterson

Jose Garcia

Grayland and Joni Noah

Candice Myers

Casablanca Press

Lou Lamoriello

Jim Harris

Arlene Ball

Dallas Cowboys

New Jersey Devils

Houston Rockets Players

Houston Aeros

Judy Nichols

Tony & Donna Vallone

Marti Boone

Roxanne Vacles

Rubin & Son

Nick Mills

Mr. & Mrs. Riccardo V.
Antona Sr.

Table of Contents

Preface

BUYING a diamond may be one of the most important purchases of your life. Think of it. If you are a man, you're probably selecting a diamond to present to your bride-to-be as a shining symbol of eternal love. Only a diamond can say it all: your love for her is clear, pure, brilliant, perfect and indestructible. If you're a woman buying a diamond for the most important man in your life, the symbolism is much the same. The diamond says, "You are the one."

For most people, the engagement ring is the first, and surely the most important, diamond they will ever buy. Selecting the right diamond, therefore, is a big responsibility. Let's make sure you get it right!

Yes, diamonds are romance, the highest expression of love, glamour, elegance, wealth and refinement. (No one ever sang, "cubic zirconias are a girl's best friend!") But diamonds are also a commodity, and there are different grades of diamonds, and each grade has a different value. And – very importantly – dealers are trying to make as much money from you as they can. You know the old expression, "A fool and his money are soon parted." Nowhere is that more true than in the diamond market. Diamond dealers can fool you in a hundred ways. Don't be fooled! In this book, I'll teach you how to judge diamonds so that when you make that all-important purchase, you get your money's worth.

Foreword

by Gregory J.P. Godek

I'M proud to introduce you to Fred Cuellar. He's not only a jeweler, he's an educator. He not only advises the Saudi royal family on their gemstone investments, he also advises guys buying their first diamond engagement ring. He not only runs a cutting house, he's an outrageous entrepreneur. He's not only the creator of the most expensive toy in the world (the $1.2 million 15th Anniversary Rubik's Cube), he's also the creator of simple yet elegant diamond engagement rings. He's not a typical, quiet jeweler, he's a frequent guest on radio and TV, including Donahue and The Today Show. He not only creates jewelry for Harley Davidson, many professional sports teams and lots of celebrities, he also creates jewelry for regular folks like you and me. He's not only a sought-after lecturer, he's now a bestselling author. He's not only the creator of the 1996 Superbowl rings for the Dallas Cowboys, he's also the creator of diamond rings that grace the hands of thousands of men and women throughout the world. He's not just any jeweler, he's a maverick who imports his own diamonds. He's not only a creative genius when it comes to jewelry, he's also a sensitive advisor who understands people's feelings as they make a very emotional and meaningful purchase. And he's not only recognized as one of the world's leading diamond experts, he's also a regular guy.

You'll learn all this as you read this awesome book. You'll also learn how to be a wise and discriminating diamond customer, a person who won't be intimidated by jewelers or diamond brokers—or by friends who think they know all about diamonds. You'll learn how to choose the perfect diamond: one that reflects your love (as well as your newfound knowledge of diamonds!). And you'll learn how to save money in the process. That's a lot to get out of one little book, isn't it?

Fred's book speaks for itself, but I'd like to add my personal guarantee. I guarantee you that the right diamond for your loved one will have a significant impact on your relationship. Diamonds really are the perfect gift of love.

Congratulations on acquiring this book. You will find that it is not only a great investment, but it is also fun to read, easy to understand, and at the same time wise and witty. Enjoy!

> ~ Gregory J.P. Godek
> author, *1001 Ways To Be Romantic*

About the Author

FRED Cuellar is founder and president of Diamond Cutters International, one of America's few diamond houses open to the public by appointment only. Mr. Cuellar's clients include some of the world's wealthiest families, including the Saudi Royal Family and a Thai princess. He is the jeweler to the Super Bowl Champion Dallas Cowboys, the Houston Aeros, Houston Rockets, New Jersey Devils, and many other professional sports teams. His private clients include hundreds of professional athletes and celebrities. Mr. Cuellar is certified in diamonds by the Gemological Institute of America, and is ranked as one of the top diamond experts in America by the *National Jeweler*. He and his wife live in Houston.

Some Highlights of Fred Cuellar's Career:

- Created the 1996 Super Bowl Championship rings for the Dallas Cowboys.
- Created the "world's most expensive toy," a full-size, fully working Rubik's Cube covered with 185 carats of precious gems.

- Created the "Million Dollar Puck" for the Houston Aeros.

- Created the "Harley of Gold," a gold-and-diamond scale replica of a Harley-Davidson motorcycle.

- Created the Baseball Bracelet for the Houston Astros.

- Created the championship rings for the 1994 NBA Champion Houston Rockets.

- Appeared on the Today Show, CBS Morning News, CNN, ESPN, PBS, Jenny Jones, the Donahue Show, and dozens of other news and talk shows.

- Advised National Jeweler Magazine, Prime Time Live, USA Today and CNN.

What people are saying about Fred Cuellar:

- "Pure genius!" Erno Rubik, inventor of Rubik's Cube

- "Simply fantastic!" Jim Harris, co-founder, Compaq Computers

- "He's what people are talking about." USA Today

- "He knows more about diamonds than I know about romance!" Greg Godek, author of *1001 Ways to be Romantic*

- "Saved me thousands on my diamond purchase!" Doug Brown, Hoboken, NJ

- "Fred, you are indeed the man who makes dreams come true!" Neal Talmadge, Director of Corporate Sales, Houston Aeros

Introduction

MY first experience with diamonds, long before I became a gemologist and diamond merchant, happened for the best of all reasons: I was a young man in love, with a burning desire to offer my bride-to-be a diamond ring and ask for her hand in marriage. It seemed simple enough. Between college classes I would stop by a jewelry store, select a diamond worthy of my beloved, and be on my way. I thought it would be easy – and it was, until I glanced at my first price tag.

After I was resuscitated by the jeweler, I realized this wasn't going to be as easy as I thought. The only "rock" I could afford then was one I could pick up off the ground.

That experience, however, led to a management trainee position with a major jewelry chain, followed by an opportunity to run a jewelry store. Then I became a wholesaler, and over time my business evolved into what it is today, where I can practice what I preach about buying and selling diamonds.

Keeping in mind my own first experience with diamond buying,

I have always tried to teach my customers everything they should know before making their purchase. If you were planning to buy a new car or a washing machine, you'd probably read *Consumer Reports* to educate yourself before the purchase, and you'd at least want to kick the tires and look under the hood before putting your money down. That's what this book is all about. It puts you in charge of the transaction by showing you how to tell one diamond from another, what makes a diamond expensive, and what "investment grade" diamonds are. I'll also show you the tricks of the trade, how to avoid shysters – in short, how to get the most for your money.

When I first published "How to Buy a Diamond," it created quite a stir. Honest diamond dealers – and there are many – loved the book. They said to me, "Fred, we've needed this for a long time, because it's hard to compete with dealers who cheat." The *dishonest* diamond dealers – and there are many of them, too, unfortunately – hated the idea of educating consumers, of revealing the "tricks of the trade." They were the ones who made threatening phone calls, who vowed to put me out of business. "You can't do this," they warned. "You can't let the suckers (that's *you*) see behind the curtain. You'll ruin us!" So of course they threatened to ruin *me* instead, and even went so far as to make attempts on my life! Things got so bad I had to hire a bodyguard to stay at my side for a couple of years. During that time, a lot of people saw me on TV, heard me on the radio, read about me in their newspapers – and bought my book. Becoming well-known made me harder to threaten. Now I'm the jeweler to the Super Bowl Champion Dallas Cowboys, and service the diamond needs of 19 other pro sports franchises. I supply 200 jewelers with their diamonds and colored stones, supply replacement diamonds for three major insurance companies, and I'm one of just two suppliers of diamonds to the Saudi royal family. But I also provide fine diamonds to private clients, individuals who may be just like you. And what matters most to me is that I've helped thousands of ordinary people get diamonds at fair prices. Helping *you* get a good deal on a diamond is just as important to me as creating a ring for football star Deion Sanders, because it takes me back to when I was a young man in love, shopping for an engagement ring.

Read my book. Call my HelpLine if you have questions. And walk through your jeweler's door with confidence that you'll walk out with the right diamond at the right price.

The Shortcut

ALTHOUGH this book has been written and designed for ease of use, I realize that some of you may be in a bit of a hurry. If you just need a crash course on what quality diamond to buy—or want a quick refresher course on the rest of the book before you head out the door to the jeweler—go directly to Chapter 2, page 65, and read the section, *What Kind of Customer Are You?* Following the recommendations in that chapter:

- go to a reputable jewelry store
- request the quality you have selected
- get an independent appraisal guaranteeing your selection, and
- you are done

Remember, if at any point in the buying process you feel overwhelmed, intimidated, or underinformed, you can always come home and read the chapters relating to your questions. In fact, you might just want to keep this book in the car!

CHAPTER ONE

THE 4 C'S

Clarity, Color, Cut & Carat Size

D IAMONDS have been prized through the ages for their beauty and rarity. How beautiful, and how rare, are determined by the Four C's. First, let's define them.

Clarity	Color	Cut	Carat Size
This indicates how clear the diamond is, how free from blemishes and other imperfections.	Diamonds are found in a variety of colors, but in general, the whiter the better.	This refers to not only the shape of the stone, but its proportions, factors which determine the sparkle of the diamond.	This is actually the weight of the stone, not its dimensions.

The price you'll pay for a diamond depends on the four C's. They determine what I call the fifth C: *Cost.*

HOW TO BUY A DIAMOND

What Is a Diamond?

Diamonds are pure crystallized carbon, often containing minor traces of impurities. Diamonds are formed at very high pressure and very high temperatures deep in the earth, and diamond is the hardest natural substance on earth.

Before we learn how to grade the quality of a diamond and determine what it should cost, let me share some acquired wisdom about diamond buying. Don't ever lose sight of the fact that you're probably buying a diamond to make the love of your life happy. If you ask a woman what she'd like in a diamond, she's not going to say, "Honey, I want a one-and-a-half carat, VS1-F in a Class Two cut." (If she does, better rob a bank – this woman's going to be expensive!) What she *will* say is something like, "Honey, I want it to be big, clear, white and sparkly." It's your job to take those general adjectives, translate them into diamond grades, decide on a stone and get your money's worth.

Remember: Focusing on only one C will rarely satisfy anyone. You can buy a one-carat diamond for a few hundred dollars if you ignore color, cut and clarity. The idea is to find a balance.

Also Remember: Never buy a diamond that's already in a setting. The setting makes it almost impossible to examine the stone carefully. Buy the diamond first, then decide what setting to put it into.

2

The Hope Diamond

One of the most famous diamonds in history, the Hope diamond, came from India and weighed 112 3/16 carats when it was acquired around 1642 by French merchant Jean Baptiste Tavernier, who was struck by its "beautiful violet" color. He sold it to the King of France, Louis XIV, who had it recut to a 67 1/8 carat stone. The blue diamond passed through ownership by French and British royalty, famed jeweler Pierre Cartier, and U.S. socialites before it was purchased by jeweler Harry Winston along with the 94.8 carat Star of the East diamond, in 1949. In 1958 Winston donated the Hope diamond to the Smithsonian Institution, where it quickly became a star attraction.

Resettings and recuttings over the centuries reduced the Hope diamond to its present 45.52 carats, 40% of its original size. Today it is set in a spectacular pendant surrounded by 16 white diamonds, and still attracts countless admirers at the Smithsonian.

CARAT WEIGHT

When you ask someone what they want in a diamond, usually the first thing they'll say is "big." So let's talk first about carat weight.

What is a "carat"? We already know it's a measure of weight, not size, but it's also a word with a fascinating history. Carat is derived from carob, the bean that's often used as a chocolate substitute. Carob trees grow in the Mediterranean region, and in ancient times a diamond of one carat, or carob, was equal in weight to a single bean, or seed, of the carob tree. In the Far East, rice was used – four grains equalled one carob bean. Eventually the carat was standardized at 200 milligrams (1/5 of a gram), and the grain was standardized at 50 milligrams. Sometimes you will hear a diamond dealer refer to a one-carat diamond as a "four-grainer."

Diamond Factoid

76% of all new brides in the United States will wear a diamond ring; 6% of these rings will be inherited.

Diamond weights are also referred to in points. One carat equals 100 points, so a 75-point diamond would weigh 3/4 of one carat. (It's not a diamond with 75 points on it, as some people think!)

The "Magical" One Carat

You've no doubt heard or seen the marketing slogans, "A diamond is forever;" "Say you'd marry her all over again with a diamond anniversary ring;" and "A one carat diamond is one in a million." These all come from ad campaigns by DeBeers, the world's largest diamond conglomerate. Through their clever marketing they have established the one-carat diamond as the minimum size to buy. That's one reason for the substantial price jump when a diamond reaches one carat. Another reason is that a good one-carat diamond *is* one in a million. But don't be swayed by advertising. There's no magic in size, and the average diamond purchased in the U.S. is 38 points – just over 1/3 of a carat.

Big Diamonds!

The biggest diamond ever found in the world is the Cullinan diamond from South Africa: 3,106 carats.

The biggest diamond ever found in the United States is the Uncle Sam from Arkansas: 40 carats.

On May 17, 1995, a flawless 100.10 carat diamond was sold by Sotheby's in Geneva for $16.5 million, the highest price ever paid at auction for a diamond.

CLARITY

The clarity of a diamond depends on how clear or "clean" it is — how free it is of blemishes and inclusions, when viewed with the naked eye and with a 10X loupe, or magnifier. Let's define our terms.

Blemishes - Imperfections on the *outside* of a diamond.

Chip:	A little piece missing, caused by wear or the cutting process.
Scratch:	A line or abrasion.
Fracture:	A crack on the diamond's surface.
Polishing lines:	Fine lines on the stone's surface formed during the polishing stage.
Natural:	An unpolished part of the diamond.
Extra facets:	Additional polished surfaces that shouldn't be there and spoil the symmetry of a diamond.
Bearding:	Very small fractures on an edge of the diamond.

Inclusions - Imperfections *inside* a diamond.

Carbon:	Black spots inside a stone.
Feather:	Internal cracking.
Crystal:	White spots inside a stone.
Pinpoint:	Tiny spots, smaller than a crystal.
Cloud:	A group of pinpoints, which may give the impression of a single large inclusion.

Loupe - (pronounced "loop") a small magnifying glass used to view gemstones. Any good jeweler will let you use one, and show you how. They should be 10X, or 10-power magnification, and the housing around the lens should be black so as not to distort the color of the stone. The Federal Trade Commission requires diamond grading to be done with a 10X magnifier, and any flaw that can't be seen under 10X magnification is considered nonexistent.

Here are the clarity grades of diamonds, as established by the Gemological Institute of America (GIA):

Flawless

Free from inclusions and blemishes when viewed under 10X magnification. *Very rare and very expensive.*

Internally Flawless

Free from inclusions; may have slight blemishes when viewed under 10X magnification. *Also very rare and very expensive.*

VVS1 and VVS2 (Very, Very Slightly Included)

Has minute inclusions or blemishes the size of a pinpoint when viewed under 10X magnification. *Rare and expensive.*

VS1 and VS2 (Very Slightly Included)

Has inclusions or blemishes smaller than a grain of salt when viewed under 10X magnification. No carbon, fractures or breaks. *High quality.*

7

SI1 (Slightly Included)

Has inclusions or blemishes larger than a grain of salt when viewed under 10X magnification, and these inclusions can be carbon or fractures. Almost all SI1 diamonds are "eye-clean," which means the flaws can't be seen with the naked eye. *Good quality.*

SI2 (Slightly Included)

Has inclusions or blemishes larger than a grain of salt when viewed under 10X magnification, and some of these flaws may be visible to the naked eye. *Borderline diamond.*

I1 (Imperfect)

Has inclusions and blemishes visible to the naked eye. *Commercial grade. Not my taste!*

I2 (Imperfect)

Has inclusions and blemishes visible to the naked eye that can make as much as one-fourth of the diamond appear cloudy and lifeless. *Same as above.*

I3 (Imperfect)

Has many, many inclusions and blemishes visible to the naked eye. Not a pretty diamond. Very little luster or sparkle. *Bottom of the barrel.*

Fred's Advice: Aim for an SI1 diamond. Many people unwittingly buy I1 and I2 stones, but if you shop carefully you can buy an SI1 stone for the same price that most I2 stones are sold for.

HOW TO SPOT CLARITY GRADES

Note: All plottings that follow show what inclusions and blemishes look like in the different clarity grades when viewed under 10X magnification.

In the plotting of the flawless diamond, you will notice there are no marks, meaning the diamond has no inclusions or blemishes.

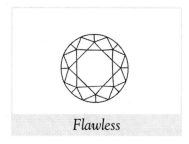

Flawless

In the plottings of the internally flawless diamond, there are no inclusions. But you will notice the slight markings representing slight blemishes.

IF (Internally Flawless)
Scratch

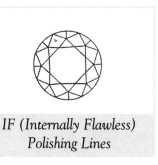

IF (Internally Flawless)
Polishing Lines

In the VVS plottings, you'll see some very minor inclusions and blemishes.

VVS1
(Very, Very Slightly Included)
Pinpoint

VVS1
(Very, Very Slightly Included)
Pinpoints, Extra Facet

VVS1
(Very, Very Slightly Included)
Pinpoints, Extra Facet

VVS1
(Very, Very Slightly Included)
Pinpoints, Scratch, Bearding

Important Note: An untrained person will have a very difficult or impossible time trying to find the inclusions or blemishes in a VVS1, or VVS2, internally flawless, or flawless diamond. Unless you're a gemologist, don't expect to. These top four grades will appear, to the average person, perfectly clean. You should only be purchasing one of these grades if you're buying the diamond for investment purposes. In my opinion, these grades are too high a quality to be worn. That would be like circulating a proof coin: it would ruin your investment.

Diamonds can get abrasions or even chipped through normal wear and tear. Some people find this hard to believe. They say that since a diamond is the hardest thing in the world, that must mean it's very tough and cannot be damaged. The truth is that even though a diamond is hard (hardness being a stone's resistance to being scratched, and the only thing that can scratch a diamond is another diamond), that doesn't mean a diamond is tough (toughness being a stone's resistance to breakage). You see, a diamond can cleave in four directions, meaning it can be damaged.

A diamond is the hardest thing in the world, but not the toughest. And it is possible for someone to buy a VVS, or flawless, diamond and through normal wear lower the clarity grade to a VS or even an SI grade. I don't recommend wearing such a high grade diamond, but if you do decide to buy one of these grades, I highly recommend that the diamond purchase be accompanied by a GIA certificate.* The GIA certificate will be your only guarantee that you are truly getting one of these grades.

*A report from a Gemological Institute of America laboratory grading the four C's of a diamond.

11

In the VS plottings, the pinpoints become a little easier to see. Also, we start to see some of the other types of inclusions and blemishes.

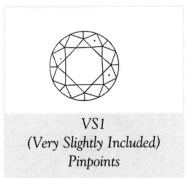

VS1
(Very Slightly Included)
Pinpoints

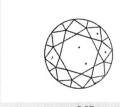

VS1
(Very Slightly Included)
Pinpoints, Bearding, Feather

VS1
(Very Slightly Included)
Pinpoints, Extra Facet, Feather

VS2
(Very Slightly Included)
Pinpoints, Crystal

VS2
(Very Slightly Included)
Pinpoints, Crystal,
Cloud, Scratch

VS2
(Very Slightly Included)
Pinpoints, Crystal,
Feathers, Scratch

In the SI plottings, we start to see larger crystals, pinpoints, feathers and the introduction of carbon.

SI1
(Slightly Included)
Pinpoints, Feathers

SI1
(Slightly Included)
Pinpoints, Carbon,
Feathers, Cloud

SI1
(Slightly Included)
Pinpoints, Carbon, Feathers

SI2
(Slightly Included)
Carbon, Crystals,
Pinpoints, Feathers

SI2
(Slightly Included)
Pinpoints, Carbon,
Feather,Crystals

SI2
(Slightly Included)
Chip, Carbon, Crystals

In the imperfect plottings, I get an opportunity to really do some drawing! You will see every type of inclusion and blemish in these grades.

I1
(Imperfect Carbon)
Feathers, Crystals, Pinpoints

I1
(Imperfect Carbon)
Carbon, Pinpoints,
Fracture, Bearding

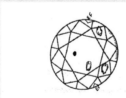

I1
(Imperfect Carbon)
Carbon, Crystals,
Bearding, Extra Facets

I2
(Imperfect Carbon)
Pinpoints, Major Feathers,
Carbon, Fractures

I2
(Imperfect Carbon)
Carbon, Major Feathers,
Chips, Clouds

I2
(Imperfect Carbon)
Crystals, Chips, Clouds,
Fractures

17

I3
(Imperfect)
Chips, Carbon, Major
Feathers, Crystals, Pinpoints

I3
(Imperfect)
Major Feathers, Bearding,
Crystals, Clouds,
Fracture Chips

I3
(Imperfect)
Clouds, Crystals, Pinpoints,
Carbon, Fracture Chips

> Fake Grade
>
> European Gem Laboratory recently introduced a "new" grade of diamond. They call it an SI3. All it really is, is an I1 diamond with a PR agent! If someone tries to sell you an SI3, don't be fooled. It's just an imperfect stone.

COLOR

Diamonds come in virtually all colors of the rainbow, from the "beautiful violet" of the Hope diamond to shades of blue, brown, gray, orange, etc. But colored diamonds are very rare and precious. Chances are, all the diamonds you'll see in your diamond shopping will be white or yellow, and the whiter the better. The yellow color in diamonds comes from nitrogen, and as a rule, the more yellow the stone, the less value it has. There's a good reason for this. The yellower the stone, the less sharp and sparkly it appears. A whiter stone lets more light pass through it, making it sparkle and shine. The exception to the rule is the *canary diamond*, which is a beautiful bright yellow and very expensive.

Some people are more sensitive to the color of diamonds. What may appear slightly yellow to you may look clear to another person, so it will take a higher color grade to satisfy you.

The best way to judge the color of a diamond is to compare it to a master set. A master set of diamonds has been graded in a laboratory. Ask the jeweler for a set, and compare the diamonds you're thinking of buying with the diamonds in the master set.

Fred's Advice: Go for grades H or I. Once mounted they'll look just as good to the average person as the higher grades, without costing a bundle. The average diamond purchased in the U.S. is color grade M or N, but the customer is usually told it's higher.

Here's the GIA Color Grading Scale:

D, E, F	Colorless
G, H, I	Nearly colorless
J, K, L	Slightly yellow
M, N, O	Light yellow
P, Q, R, S, T, U, V, W, X	Darker yellow
Z	Fancy colors

Even though there are several grades in each category, there are slight differences between the letter grades. D is the clearest and most valuable, X is a dingy yellow and least expensive. Z grade — colored diamonds — are the rarest and most expensive. A diamond so saturated with nitrogen that it becomes a deep, rich yellow is as rare as a colorless diamond.

❧ Quick and Easy Grading Tips ❧

Clarity

1) If you can see any inclusions or blemishes with your own eyes, the diamond is no better than I1.

2) With a 10X loupe, if you see *any* black spots, cracks, or anything larger than a grain of salt, the diamond is no better than SI1.

3) With a 10X loupe, if you can see *nothing* wrong with the diamond, only then could it be a VS1 or VS2.

Color

Take a pure white business card. Fold it in half. Lay the diamond in the crease. If you pick up *any yellow* the diamond is no better than K.

More About Color: Fluorescence

Fluorescence is a diamond's reaction to ultraviolet (UV) light. Some diamonds glow in different colors under UV light, and the general rule is to avoid them. If you put a diamond under UV light and it glows strong blue, the diamond may look dull in the sunlight. Diamonds with strong fluorescence may be worth up to 20% less than diamonds which do not fluoresce. Faint fluorescence which doesn't fog the diamond is OK.

❧ **Diamond Myth** ❧

"Yellow diamonds are worthless"

Yellow diamonds *are* worth less than white diamonds, but they still have value. And if a diamond contains so much nitrogen that it's very bright yellow, it can be worth quite a bit. Bright yellow diamonds are known as "canary diamonds," and they're more valuable than light yellow diamonds.

Corresponding Grading

Corresponding grading means matching clarity grades with color grades. For every clarity grade, there's a color grade that *corresponds*, or makes the best match in determining value. Diamonds that have corresponding grading sell for higher prices originally, and they also appreciate in value more than diamonds that don't, and therefore have higher resale value. Buying a diamond with non-corresponding clarity and color grades is like buying a pink Porsche: it's okay as long as you don't try to resell it. The market for pink Porsches just isn't as good as the market for, say, red Porsches.

Here's a list of clarity grades and their corresponding color grades. Notice that for each clarity grade there's a *perfect* match, and a high and low color that also works well.

CLARITY GRADE	COLOR GRADE	ANNUAL INCREASE IN $ VALUE
Flawless and Internally Flawless	D (Perfect) E (Low)	10.00%
VVS1, VVS2	D (High) E (Perfect) F (Low)	9.25%
VS1, VS2	F (High) G (Perfect) H (Low)	8.50%
SI1, SI2	H (High) I (Perfect) J (Low)	6.50%
Lower	No corresponding color grades	

The value of a stone is always based on the *lowest* clarity or color grade and its highest corresponding grade. For example: Let's say you purchased a stone with a clarity grade of SI1 and a color grade of G. You can see above that G is not a corresponding color for an SI1 stone. The SI1-G diamond will cost you more than the SI1-H, but will appreciate no more over time than the SI1-H.

When you *don't* correspond the grades – say, you buy high clarity and low color, or high color and low clarity – you'll never get your money back for the higher grade. For example, an SI1-F would resell no higher than the value of an SI1-H, and a VS1-I would resell no higher than the value of an SI1-I.

A diamond that is *not* correspondingly-graded could be expected to appreciate 2% to 4% per year.

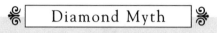

Diamond Myth

"Diamonds Are Indestructible"

False! Diamonds are the hardest natural substance known on earth, but they are not the toughest. There's a difference between the hardness and the toughness of materials. A sharp blow can certainly damage your diamond.

CUT

Okay, we're three-fourths of the way to becoming diamond experts! We've learned to check the carat weight of a diamond. We know how diamonds are graded for clarity, and how to look for a diamond that's "clean." We also know that diamonds range from D to X, "colorless" to "darker yellow," on the color scale. Now we'll learn about the fourth C: Cut.

The first thing to know is that the cut of a diamond indicates more than its shape. The cut also determines how *sparkly* your diamond will be!

It's not enough that a diamond is big and clear and white. No diamond can be truly attractive unless it *sparkles*, and it won't sparkle unless it's properly cut. You can buy a one-carat diamond, graded SI2 or higher for clarity, and rated J or better on the color scale, and it *still* won't sparkle unless the cut is good.

To understand what I mean, first let's look at some shapes. Diamonds can be cut into a wide variety of shapes. Shown on the following pages are some of the most popular.

Off-Makes

This is the number one problem with diamonds! An "off-make" is a poorly-proportioned diamond, and no matter how white, how clean or how big a diamond is, it won't achieve maximum sparkle, fire and brilliance unless it's cut correctly. Always make sure a diamond is well proportioned by following the Proportion Questionnaire Sheet guidelines. (p. 43)

MODERN DIAMOND CUTS

Box Radiant

Marquise or Navette

Pear

Standard Radiant

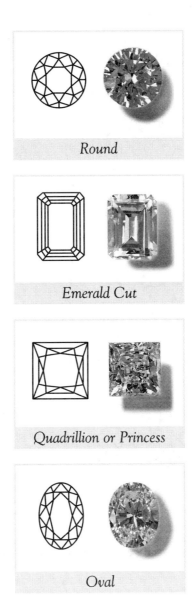

Round

Emerald Cut

Quadrillion or Princess

Oval

OLD ERA DIAMOND CUTS

The old era or non-modern cuts tend to be off-make, or poorly proportioned diamonds.

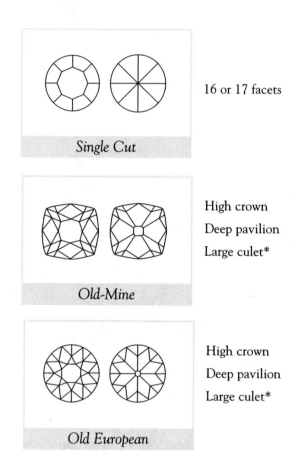

Single Cut — 16 or 17 facets

Old-Mine — High crown / Deep pavilion / Large culet*

Old European — High crown / Deep pavilion / Large culet*

*Creates appearance of a hole in the center of the diamond, when viewed from above.

Now that you've had a look at some diamond shapes, let's go over the parts of the cut diamond.

There are three basic parts to every cut diamond: The crown (top), the girdle (around the middle), and the pavilion (the bottom).

The crown consists of a large flat area on top called the table, and a number of facets. As the diamond catches the light, the job of the crown is to split the light entering the diamond into *white light*, which gives the stone its brilliance, and colored light, which gives it fire, or dispersion.

The girdle is the thin, unpolished band around the widest part of the diamond. The function of the girdle is to protect the edge of the stone from chipping (even though diamond is the hardest natural substance on earth, it can be chipped!).

The pavilion has the most important job, which is to reflect the light that passes through the crown back into your eyes. Think of it as a cone lined with mirrors. The light enters the diamond through the crown, splits into white and colored light, bounces off the facets of the pavilion back up through the crown, where you see it as – *sparkle!*

But to achieve the maximum sparkle – that magic combination of brilliance and fire – the diamond must be well cut *and* cut in the proper proportions. The size of the table, the symmetry of the facets, the thickness of the girdle, and the angle of the pavilion must all work together to give the diamond the sparkle you want.

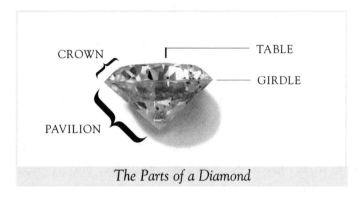

CROWN

TABLE

GIRDLE

PAVILION

The Parts of a Diamond

Let's take these areas one at a time to see how they affect the quality of the diamond.

Table

The size of the table, as a percentage of the crown, is important because it determines the amount of *brilliance*, or white light, the diamond will reflect. For example, if the table is 60% of the area of the crown, 60% of the light you see will be *brilliance* and 40% will be *fire*, or dispersion. *Avoid a diamond with a table area of 65% or higher.* It will give the diamond too much brilliance, and not enough fire – and the diamond will look fuzzy or foggy.

Here's the formula:

Table area 53-58% = GREAT!
Table area 59-64% = GOOD!
Table area 65%+   = AVOID!

So how do you determine exactly what the table area is? It's obviously a measurement that's pretty difficult to make unless you have the right instruments. You may not be able to measure it, but from the table above you know what it should be – so, *ask the dealer!* And tell the dealer you'll have his answer checked by an independent appraiser, so he might as well tell you the truth.

Diamonds in the Rough

An uncut diamond, as it is found in nature, is called "rough." As a rule of thumb, it takes a three-carat rough to produce a good quality one-carat cut stone. Often, poorly-proportioned diamonds are the result of a diamond cutter trying to make a one-carat stone from a two-carat rough.

Facets

The typical diamond is cut with 58 facets, 33 on the crown and 25 on the pavilion. On a well-proportioned stone, these facets will be uniform and symmetrical. If they are not, the diamond's ability to refract and reflect light will suffer. Furthermore, a poorly-cut diamond just won't look right to the eye. The sad fact is, *75% of all rounds and 88% of all other shapes on the market are poorly proportioned!* Poorly proportioned stones are more profitable for the dealer, because they retain more of the weight of the "rough" or uncut diamond. That allows the dealer to sell it as a bigger diamond than it should be, and get more money for it, even though it sparkles less. *Look closely! Choose a diamond that's well cut, even if you have to search a while to find it.*

31

Girdle

This is a Goldilocks problem. You don't want a diamond with a girdle that's too thin, or one that's too thick – you want one that's just right! The whole purpose of the girdle is to protect the edge of the stone from chipping. A girdle that's too thin doesn't give enough protection. A girdle that's too thick *does* protect against chipping, but it doesn't look so good. So you want a diamond with a medium girdle, neither too thin nor too thick. How do you tell? Look at the diamond from the side. If it looks like there's a white chalk line around the middle of the stone, the girdle is too thick. If you don't see any girdle at all with the naked eye, look at the same area of the stone with a 10X loupe. If you can't see a girdle with the loupe, it's too thin.

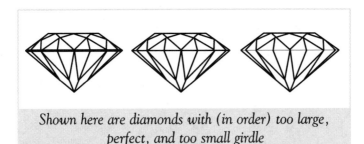

Shown here are diamonds with (in order) too large, perfect, and too small girdle

Pavilion

The job of the pavilion is most important of all: to reflect light into your True Love's eyes. I think it's important to understand that when you look at a diamond and see it sparkle, you're not just seeing light reflected off the surface of the diamond.

The light enters the diamond through the table and the facets of the crown, passes through the diamond, and is reflected back by the facets of the pavilion.

Here's the important part: The angle of the pavilion for a round diamond must be exactly 40.75 degrees. For fancy shapes, the perfect angle is 40 degrees, but an acceptable range is 39.25 - 40.75 degrees.

If the pavilion angle is *not* exactly right it will not reflect the light properly, and the diamond won't have the sparkle it should. In a round diamond, there's a dramatic loss of sparkle if the angle is even a quarter of a degree above or below 40.75 degrees. In fancy shapes, maximum sparkle is achieved with a 40 degree pavilion angle, but the angle can be increased or decreased by as much as three-fourths of a degree with only a 10% loss of sparkle.

As I mentioned, 88% of fancy shapes are poorly cut. A great many people in the diamond industry believe that if that many are cut wrong, it must make it right. It doesn't! Some even argue that the angle can't be accurately measured on a fancy shape. Wrong! You simply measure the pavilion angle at the diamond's widest point. GIA has relaxed its guidelines for fancy shapes, but you and I have not! Insist on the correct angle, and if you don't get it, keep looking.

Crown Angle

The angle of the crown is also important, but it doesn't have to be quite as precise as the pavilion angle. *The angle of the crown should be 32 - 34 1/2 degrees.* If it's smaller than 32 degrees, the diamond is what we call "spread-cut." This makes the table area too large and the girdle too thin, and we already know what problems that causes.

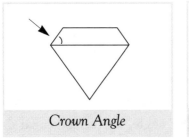

Crown Angle

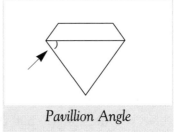

Pavillion Angle

If the angle of the crown is *above* 34 1/2 degrees, it makes the diamond "top heavy." This results in a smaller diameter, making the diamond look smaller than it really is. The last thing you want is a one-carat diamond that looks like a 3/4 carat!

Culet

Finally, at the very bottom of the diamond – the base of the pavilion – there may be a small facet called the culet. If this facet is too large, when you look straight down through the table it will look like the diamond has a hole in the middle. *Make sure the stone has no culet or a very small culet.*

❀ | Buying Tip | ❀

If a diamond dealer can't (or won't) answer your questions, assume the worst! For example, if the dealer can't tell you the girdle thickness, assume it's too thin or too thick. If the dealer can't tell you the crown angle, assume it's below 32 degrees and the diamond is spread-cut.

Two Other Important Diamond Measurements

Two other measurements to consider are total depth and length-to-width ratio.

Total depth is a simple, straightforward measurement: take the height of the stone and divide it by the diameter of the stone. For a fancy stone, the diameter is measured at its widest part. The answer should be in the 59.3% - 61% range. If it's not, it means there's something wrong with the crown angle and/or the pavilion angle, or the girdle thickness.

The *length-to-width ratio* is used to determine if a fancy-shaped diamond (anything other than round) is well-proportioned. For example, we don't want to buy a marquise that is so skinny it looks like a banana, or one that's so fat it looks like a football.

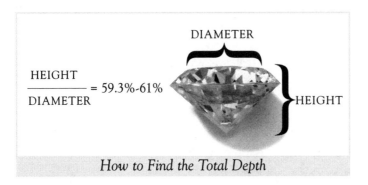

$$\frac{HEIGHT}{DIAMETER} = 59.3\%\text{-}61\%$$

How to Find the Total Depth

Pleasing proportions aside, the length-to-width ratio also affects a phenomenon known as the *bow-tie*. Let me explain. *Fancy shapes are not symmetrical – only a round is.* And because fancy

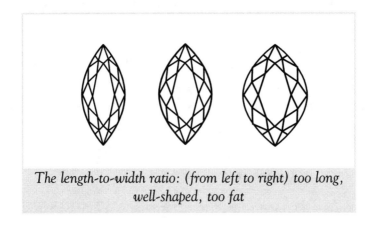

The length-to-width ratio: (from left to right) too long, well-shaped, too fat

stones aren't symmetrical, they all have a bow-tie – two triangular shadows in the middle of the diamond where light leaks out the bottom.

If the length-to-width ratio is off, it will intensify the bow-tie in the stone!

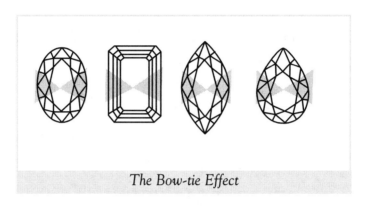

The Bow-tie Effect

For a marquise diamond, the length should be no less than 1.75 times the width, and no more than 2 times the width.

For pear, emerald and oval shapes, the length should be no less than 1.5 times the width, and no more than 1.75 times the width.

PROPORTIONS MADE EASY

GIA has made it easier to determine if a diamond is well-proportioned by dividing all cut diamonds into four classes.

Essentially, *Class One* and *Class Two* diamonds are well-proportioned; *Class Three* and *Class Four* diamonds are not (see page 41-42).

Class One diamonds are investment-quality stones, beautifully proportioned and priced to match. For a stone to be rated Class

One is like getting an A+ on a test. Class Two diamonds get a straight A on the same test, and if your objective is to buy a beautiful diamond to wear, Class Two is fine.

Fred's Advice: Don't go below Class Two. And if the jeweler doesn't know what the GIA classes are – move on!

❧ Diamond Myth ❧

"A fancy-shaped diamond is more difficult to cut and more valuable than a round diamond"

Actually, a fancy shape is no more difficult to cut than a round diamond, and a round diamond is generally the most expensive shape simply because of demand. 65% of all diamonds sold are round. The emerald cut can be the least expensive because its shape is most like the natural shape of the *rough* – the uncut diamond.

PROPORTION AND PRICE

Here's an example of what proportion can mean to price: Let's say you go to two different jewelry stores, Joe's and Mike's. They are both offering a round, 1carat, VS1-G diamond.

Joe's Price: $6,200

Mike's Price: $4,900

Immediately you notice that Joe's price is $1,300 higher than Mike's. This could be because Joe is just trying to make more money on the same quality diamond. But you look more closely at the diamonds, and discover that Joe's diamond is well proportioned, and Mike's is poorly proportioned. So in this case you should buy at Joe's. You're getting your money's worth.

A poorly proportioned diamond is worth as much as 40% less than a well proportioned stone.

One reason for the difference in worth is that it takes a 3-carat "rough," which is a diamond as it's found in nature, to produce a well proportioned 1-carat cut stone. But it only takes a 2-carat rough to produce a poorly proportioned 1-carat stone.

But, you say, one carat is one carat! What's the big deal?

The big deal is that a poorly proportioned diamond will not sparkle nearly as much as a well proportioned diamond. If a diamond is poorly proportioned, only 35-40% of the light that enters it will reflect back up into your True Love's eyes, while a well proportioned diamond will reflect close to 90% of the light. A woman wants a diamond to be "big, clean, white and sparkly," and it won't sparkle unless it's well proportioned.

Well, there you have it – the basics of judging diamond quality: CARAT WEIGHT, CLARITY, COLOR AND CUT. You're well on your way to becoming a savvy diamond buyer.

Diamond Lore

Diamonds have been treasured throughout history for their special qualities, but for most of that time they have been very rare, and available only to the super-rich. Not until after the discovery of large diamond deposits in South Africa around 1865 did diamonds become plentiful enough to be affordable to people of more modest means. In fact, now diamonds are not rare at all! The market for diamonds is carefully controlled by the big diamond cartels to keep prices artificially high.

GIA CLASSES OF CUTS

Class I American/Tolkowsky Cut (15% above cost)*

Table %	53% of diameter of stone
Total depth	59.3% of diameter of stone
Crown angle	34.5 degrees
Crown height	16.2% of diameter of stone
Girdle thickness	.7-1.7%of diameter of stone
Pavilion angle	40.75 degrees for rounds; 39.25 to 40.75 degrees for all other shapes
Pavilion depth	43.1% of diameter of stone

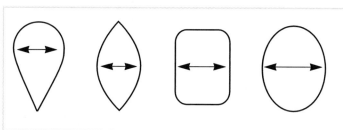

The diameter of any shaped diamond other than round is the diamond's maximum width

Class II (Cost)*

Table %	53-64%
Crown angles	32-34.5 degrees
Girdle thickness	Thin to thick (medium preferred)
Pavilion angle	40.75 degrees for rounds; 39.25 to 40.75 degrees for all other shapes
Polish & symmetry	Good

Class III (15-25% below cost)*

Table %	65-70%
Crown angles	30-32 degrees
Girdle thickness	Very thin or very thick
Pavilion angle	Any measurement other than 40.75 degrees for rounds or 39.25 to 40.75 degrees for all other shapes
Polish & symmetry	Fair to good

Class IV (50-60% below cost)*

Table %	70% and above
Crown angles	30 degrees and below
Girdle thickness	Very thin or very thick
Pavilion angle	Any measurement other than 40.75 degrees for rounds or 39.25 to 40.75 degrees for all other shapes
Polish & symmetry	Fair to poor

*Cost refers to the price guide in this book.

PROPORTION QUESTIONNAIRE SHEET (P.Q.S): A WORKSHEET

Now that you know what you're looking for, here's a quick questionnaire that will tell you if a stone measures up.

_____ 1. What is the table?

53-58%	(1 pt)
59-64%	(0 pt)
65%+	(-1 pt)

_____ 2. What is the crown angle?

32-34.5 degrees	(1 pt)
Above 34.5 degrees	(0 pt)
Below 32 degrees	(-1 pt)

_____ 3. What is the height of the crown?

14.2% to 16.2% of diameter	(1 pt)
Above 16.2%	(0 pt)
Below 14.2%	(-1 pt)

_____ 4. What is the pavilion angle?

      40.75 degrees (round diamond)   (1 pt)

      39.25 to 40.75 degrees (fancy shapes)   (1 pt)

      Anything else   ·   (Disqualification)

_____ 5. What is the pavilion depth?

      43.1% of diameter   (1 pt)

      Anything else   (Disqualification)

_____ 6. What is the total depth percentage?

      59-61%   (1 pt)

      Above 61%   (0 pt)

      Below 59%   (-1 pt)

_____ 7. What is the girdle thickness?

      Medium   (1 pt)

      Thick   (0 pt)

      Thin to very thin   (-1 pt)

_____ 8. What is the culet size?

      None or small   (1 pt)

      Medium or large   (-1 pt)

_____ 9. Is the cutting of the stone symmetrical?

      Excellent or good   (1 pt)

      Fair or poor   (-1 pt)

_____ 10. What GIA class of cut is the diamond?

      1 or 2   (1 pt)

      3 or 4   (Disqualification)

_____ 11. How is the polish?

      Excellent or good   (1 pt)

      Fair to poor   (-1 pt)

For the diamond to pass proportionately it must not disqualify and must have a score of 6+ points.

HOW TO BUY A DIAMOND

CHAPTER TWO

COST

The Fifth "C"

―――――――――――

OKAY, time to talk real money. The prices listed here are the latest *wholesale* diamond prices at the time this book went to press. These are approximate prices, but because the supply of diamonds is so carefully controlled by the international diamond cartels, prices don't fluctuate very much. You can expect prices to rise no more than 5% a year on average.

How Much to Spend

I'm sure you have heard the rule of thumb that says you should spend two-months' salary on a diamond engagement ring. Well, let's not forget whose thumb we're talking about here: *the diamond cartel's*. There is no magic in that guideline — it wasn't given to Moses on a tablet, it's not in the Bible or the Dead Sea Scrolls. It's a marketing gimmick aimed at getting you to spend as much money as possible for your diamond. Don't be bullied by the diamond industry into buying something you can't afford! You should examine your own budget carefully and decide what you can afford.

Even if you *do* use the two-months' salary guideline, if you follow my advice and buy wisely, you'll only have to spend *one*-month's salary to get what an uneducated buyer would pay double for.

Keep in mind as you look through the price chart that the *price per carat* increases with the size of the diamond. For example, a half-carat VS1-G costs $2,150, or $4,300 per carat, while an actual one-carat VS1-G costs $6,200. That's because the larger stones are rarer.

If you do your homework and shop around, you should be able to buy a diamond at these prices. If you have problems, call my HelpLine: (713) 22-CARAT. The HelpLine is in operation 9:00-6:00 (Central Time) Monday through Friday, and 9:00-12:00 Noon (Central Time) on Saturday.

❧ | Diamond Price Tables | ❧

1/3 carat (33 points)

COLOR	IF	VVS1	VVS2	VS1	VS2	SI1	SI2	I1	I2	I3
D	1683	1584	1485	1221	957	759	693	528	429	330
E	1584	1485	1320	1155	891	726	660	495	396	297
F	1485	1320	1221	1056	825	693	627	462	363	297
G	1287	1118	1056	957	792	660	594	429	363	264
H	990	924	858	792	693	627	561	396	330	264
I	792	759	726	693	627	594	528	396	330	264
J	693	693	660	627	561	528	495	363	330	231
K	627	594	561	528	495	462	429	363	297	231
L	561	528	561	462	462	429	396	297	264	231
M	495	495	462	429	396	396	330	264	231	231

Example: 1/3 carat, I2 (Clarity), G (Color) = $363

1/2 carat (50 points)

COLOR	IF	VVS1	VVS2	VS1	VS2	SI1	SI2	I1	I2	I3
D	4150	3400	3100	2550	2100	1800	1450	1150	900	700
E	3400	3150	2700	2400	2050	1750	1400	1100	850	650
F	3150	2750	2450	2250	2000	1650	1350	1050	800	650
G	2750	2450	2250	2150	1900	1550	1300	1000	800	600
H	2350	2150	1950	1850	1650	1500	1250	950	750	600
I	1900	1750	1650	1500	1400	1300	1200	900	750	600
J	1600	1500	1400	1350	1300	1250	1150	850	750	550
K	1300	1250	1200	1150	1100	1050	950	800	700	550
L	1250	1200	1150	1100	1050	1000	900	700	650	500
M	1050	1000	1000	950	900	850	800	650	600	450

Example: 1/2 carat, SI2 (Clarity), G (Color) = $1,300

✻ Diamond Price Tables ✻

3/4 carat (75 points)

COLOR	IF	VVS1	VVS2	VS1	VS2	SI1	SI2	I1	I2	I3
D	6675	5325	4800	4125	3600	3300	2925	2100	1500	1125
E	5325	4950	4275	3825	3450	3225	2850	2100	1500	1050
F	4875	4350	3825	3525	3375	3150	2775	2100	1425	1050
G	4275	3900	3525	3375	3225	3000	2700	2025	1425	975
H	3825	3525	3375	3225	3075	2850	2550	1950	1350	975
I	3225	3075	3000	2925	2850	2700	2400	1875	1275	975
J	2850	2700	2700	2625	2475	2325	2175	1800	1275	900
K	2550	2475	2400	2325	2175	2025	1875	1500	1200	900
L	2175	2100	2025	1950	1950	1800	1650	1200	1050	825
M	1800	1800	1725	1725	1725	1650	1500	1125	975	750

Example: 3/4 carat, VS2 (Clarity), L (Color) = $1,950

1 carat (100 points)
Clarity

COLOR	IF	VVS1	VVS2	VS1	VS2	SI1	SI2	I1	I2	I3
D	16000	11100	9600	7800	6500	5700	5100	3700	2600	1800
E	11100	9700	7800	6800	6300	5600	5000	3600	2600	1700
F	9700	8000	6900	6600	6100	5500	4900	3500	2500	1700
G	7900	7000	6500	6200	5800	5400	4800	3400	2400	1600
H	6900	6300	6000	5700	5500	5200	4600	3300	2300	1600
I	6100	5800	5500	5300	5100	4800	4300	3200	2200	1500
J	5600	5400	5200	5000	4800	4400	4000	3000	2100	1500
K	5100	4900	4800	4600	4300	4100	3700	2800	2000	1400
L	4300	4200	4100	3900	3700	3500	3300	2600	1900	1300
M	3600	3500	3400	3200	3100	2800	2600	2200	1800	1300

Example: 1 carat, VS1 (Clarity), F (Color) = $6,600

50

❧ | Diamond Price Tables | ❧

1 1/2 carat (150 points)
Clarity

COLOR	IF	VVS1	VVS2	VS1	VS2	SI1	SI2	I1	I2	I3
D	26250	18150	16500	13800	11250	9600	8700	6150	4350	2850
E	18150	16650	13950	11700	10800	9450	8250	6000	4350	2700
F	16650	14250	12150	11100	10350	9300	8100	5850	4200	2700
G	14100	12150	10950	10500	9750	9000	7950	5850	4050	2550
H	12000	10650	10050	9750	9300	8850	7650	5700	3900	2550
I	10200	9750	9300	9000	8550	7950	7200	5500	3750	2400
J	9450	9150	8700	8550	8100	7500	6750	5100	3600	2400
K	8550	8250	7950	7650	7200	6750	6150	4650	3450	2250
L	7200	6900	6750	6450	6150	5850	5400	4350	3300	2100
M	6600	5850	5700	5400	5100	4650	4350	3750	3000	2100

Example: 1 1/2 carat, VVS2 (Clarity), J (Color) = $8,700

2 carat (200 points)
Clarity

COLOR	IF	VVS1	VVS2	VS1	VS2	SI1	SI2	I1	I2	I3
D	50000	38400	33400	26400	21200	16400	13200	9000	6200	4200
E	38400	33400	26400	22800	19000	16000	13000	8800	6200	4000
F	33400	26600	23500	19600	18200	15600	12800	8600	6200	3800
G	26400	23600	19400	18200	17000	14800	12400	8400	6000	3800
H	22600	19000	17600	16600	15000	13600	11800	8200	5800	3600
I	17400	16400	15800	14200	13000	12200	11000	8000	5600	3400
J	15200	14600	13800	12800	12000	11200	10000	7800	5400	3400
K	12600	12200	11800	11400	11000	10200	9200	7200	5200	3200
L	10600	10200	9800	9400	9000	8600	8000	6600	5000	3000
M	9000	8600	8200	7800	7400	6800	6400	5600	4600	3000

Example: 2 carat, SI1 (Clarity), I (Color) = $12,200

❧ Diamond Price Tables ❧

3 carat (300 points)
Clarity

COLOR	IF	VVS1	VVS2	VS1	VS2	SI1	SI2	I1	I2	I3
D	118500	86100	72600	56100	45600	37500	27900	21000	11400	6900
E	86100	74400	56400	45600	40500	35100	26400	19500	11100	6600
F	72600	56700	45900	40500	37800	32700	25200	18300	10800	6300
G	56100	45900	40500	37800	32700	29100	23700	17400	10200	6000
H	45600	40200	36900	33000	29100	24900	22200	16200	9600	6000
I	35700	32700	31200	38400	24600	22500	19800	15000	9300	5700
J	29700	28200	27000	24600	22200	20400	18300	13800	8700	5400
K	26400	24900	23700	21600	19800	18000	15900	12900	8400	5400
L	20700	19800	18900	18000	16500	14700	12900	10500	8100	5100
M	16800	16200	15600	15000	14400	12900	11400	9300	7500	5100

Example: 3 carat, VVS1 (Clarity), H (Color) = $40,200

4 carat (400 points)
Clarity

COLOR	IF	VVS1	VVS2	VS1	VS2	SI1	SI2	I1	I2	I3
D	166000	122800	104800	80800	66800	55200	40000	30400	17200	9600
E	122800	104800	80800	66800	60000	51200	38000	28400	16800	9200
F	104800	81200	62700	58800	54800	47200	36400	26800	16000	8800
G	80800	67200	59200	54800	47600	41200	34800	24200	15600	8400
H	64800	58800	52800	47600	41600	37200	32000	23600	14800	8400
I	50800	46800	43600	41600	38400	33200	29600	22400	14000	8000
J	40800	38800	36800	34800	32800	29200	26800	20800	13200	7600
K	36000	34000	32000	30000	28000	25200	23200	18400	12400	7200
L	28800	27200	26400	25200	23600	21200	18800	15600	11600	6800
M	24000	22800	22400	21600	20800	11800	16800	14000	10800	6800

Example: 4 carat, IF (Clarity), D (Color) = $166,000

Diamond Price Tables

5 carat (500 points)
Clarity

COLOR	IF	VVS1	VVS2	VS1	VS2	SI1	SI2	I1	I2	I3
D	277500	196000	166000	138500	113500	96500	66500	41500	24500	13500
E	196000	168500	138500	118500	103500	86500	64000	39000	24000	12500
F	168500	139000	121500	106000	91000	76500	61500	37500	22500	12000
G	138500	121500	106500	91000	80000	69500	57500	35500	21500	11500
H	116000	103500	91000	80000	70500	59500	49500	33000	20500	11000
I	91000	86000	80000	69500	61500	49500	43500	30000	19500	10500
J	64000	61500	59000	56500	50000	42000	37500	27500	18500	10000
K	51500	49000	46500	44000	41500	37000	31500	25000	17500	10000
L	42000	39500	37500	35500	33000	30500	26500	22000	16000	9500
M	34500	33500	31500	30000	28500	26500	29000	19000	14500	9500

Example: 5 carat, IF (Clarity), D (Color) = $277,500

BUYING BIG DIAMONDS

If you're in the market for a larger diamond, in the 6-to-10 carat range, here's a formula to help you determine the approximate cost. These prices are based on GIA Class 2 cut or better.

1. Decide the clarity grade and the color grade you want.

2. Decide the carat weight diamond you want.

3. Go to the price list for 5-carat diamonds and find the same clarity and color grade you chose. Write down the price.

4. Divide that price by 5. This will give you the per carat price.

5. Multiply the per-carat price by the carat weight of the diamond you chose.

6. Increase that amount by the percentage listed below in the weight category you chose, and you'll have your total cost.

For example: Let's say we want a 7-carat diamond, graded VS2-G.

- We look up a 5-carat VS2-G and find the price is $80,000.

- Divide $80,000 by 5 carats and get the per-carat cost of $16,000.

- Multiply $16,000 by 7 carats, and we get $112,000.

- In the 7 carat table below, we find VS-G and see that we need to increase our cost by 8.1%.

$112,000 x .081= $9.072

$112,000 + 9,072= $121,072—The cost of our 7-carat stone.

Remember—these figures should be used only as guidelines.

The following tables show the approximate percentage of cost increase for over 5 carat stones (use formula above).

Big Diamond Price Tables

6 Carat Stones

COLOR	IF	VVS	VS	SI	I1	I2-I3
D	2.6%	2.5%	2.4%	2.3%	2.2%	2.1%
E	2.4%	2.3%	2.2%	2.3%	2.2%	2.1%
F	2.4%	2.3%	2.2%	2.1%	2.1%	2.0%
G	2.2%	2.1%	2.1%	2.1%	2.1%	2.0%
H	2.2%	2.1%	2.1%	2.0%	2.0%	2.0%
I	2.0%	2.0%	2.0%	2.0%	2.0%	1.7%
J	2.0%	2.0%	2.0%	2.0%	2.0%	1.5%
K	2.0%	2.0%	2.0%	2.0%	2.0%	1.5%
L-M	1.4%	1.3%	1.2%	1.1%	1.0%	1.0%

Big Diamond Price Tables

7 Carat Stones

COLOR	IF	VVS	VS	SI	I1	I2-I3
D	7.7%	8.6%	8.3%	8.2%	6.6%	5.9%
E	7.6%	8.6%	8.3%	8.2%	6.5%	5.8%
F	7.6%	8.5%	8.2%	8.2%	6.5%	5.7%
G	7.5%	8.5%	8.1%	8.1%	6.4%	5.6%
H	7.5%	8.5%	8.1%	8.1%	6.3%	5.6%
I	7.0%	8.4%	8.0%	8.1%	6.2%	5.5%
J	7.0%	8.3%	8.0%	8.0%	6.0%	5.5%
K	6.5%	8.2%	8.0%	8.0%	6.0%	5.5%
L-M	5.5%	5.4%	5.3%	5.2%	5.1%	5.0%

8 Carat Stones

COLOR	IF	VVS	VS	SI	I1	I2-I3
D	8.8%	10.8%	10.7%	10.3%	7.8%	6.7%
E	8.8%	10.7%	10.7%	10.3%	7.7%	6.6%
F	8.8%	10.7%	10.5%	10.3%	7.7%	6.6%
G	8.7%	10.5%	10.5%	10.1%	7.6%	6.6%
H	8.7%	10.5%	10.5%	10.1%	7.6%	6.5%
I	8.5%	10.5%	10.4%	10.0%	7.5%	6.5%
J	8.5%	10.4%	10.4%	10.0%	7.5%	6.5%
K	8.1%	10.4%	10.3%	10.0%	7.5%	6.5%
L-M	6.6%	6.5%	6.4%	6.3%	6.2%	6.1%

❧ Big Diamond Price Tables ❧

9 Carat Stones

COLOR	IF	VVS	VS	SI	I1	I2-I3
D	15.5%	18.5%	18.5%	16.4%	13.0%	11.4%
E	15.5%	18.5%	18.4%	16.3%	13.0%	11.4%
F	15.5%	18.4%	18.3%	16.3%	13.0%	11.4%
G	15.4%	18.3%	18.3%	16.2%	12.9%	11.3%
H	15.4%	18.3%	18.3%	16.2%	12.8%	11.3%
I	14.6%	18.3%	18.2%	16.2%	12.8%	11.2%
J	14.5%	18.2%	18.2%	16.1%	12.7%	11.2%
K	14.2%	18.2%	18.0%	16.0%	12.7%	11.2%
L-M	11.5%	11.4%	11.3%	11.2%	11.1%	11.1%

10 Carat Stones

COLOR	IF	VVS	VS	SI	I1	I2-I3
D	26.2%	26.2%	26.2%	26.2%	24.8%	22.5%
E	26.2%	26.1%	26.1%	26.1%	24.8%	22.5%
F	26.1%	26.1%	27.5%	27.5%	24.8%	22.4%
G	26.1%	26.1%	27.2%	27.2%	24.6%	22.3%
H	26.1%	26.0%	27.1%	27.1%	24.6%	22.2%
I	26.0%	24.5%	25.0%	25.0%	24.5%	22.1%
J	26.0%	24.5%	25.0%	25.0%	24.5%	22.0%
K	26.0%	24.5%	24.8%	24.8%	24.2%	22.0%
L-M	21.6%	21.6%	21.5%	21.5%	21.3%	21.1%

Buying Shy

"Buying shy" is a term I coined. It's one of my shrewdest and most valuable suggestions for buying diamonds. Buying shy can save you a lot of money!

Here's what I mean by buying shy: *Shopping for diamonds that weigh just under half-carat and full-carat weights.*

For example, instead of a 1-carat (100-point) diamond you'd buy a .90-carat diamond. Instead of a half-carat, you'd buy a .49-carat stone. It's as simple as that.

But Fred, you're saying – why should I buy a smaller diamond than I want?

The simple answer: to save a lot of money.

Because the price of a diamond jumps dramatically when it reaches a true half-carat or full carat, the advantage of buying shy is also pretty dramatic!

And let's see how much "smaller" we're talking about. The diameter of a 1-carat diamond is 6.5 millimeters. The diameter of a "shy" .90-carat stone is 6.3 mm. The difference is the thickness of a piece of ordinary paper! Looking at the stones side by side you'd be hard-pressed to tell the difference.

Look at the savings:

.50ct SI1-I	$1,300	
.49ct SI1-I	$1,078	You save $222!
1.00ct SI1-I	$4,800	
.90ct SI1-I	$3,330	You save $1,470!
1.50ct SI1-I	$7,950	
1.49ct SI1-I	$7,156	You save $794!
2.00ct SI1-I	$12,200	
1.90ct SI1-I	$10,070	You save $2,130!

You'll notice that buying shy sometimes means a difference of .01 point and sometimes a difference of .10 point. And you're thinking, "Why don't I buy the .99-carat stone instead of the .90 carat stone? Won't I still get the same price break and a slightly bigger stone?" Yes, but the problem is finding that 99-pointer. Diamond cutters, who are well aware that the full one-carat stone is worth quite a bit more than the 99-pointer, will cheat on the proportions a bit to get the stone up to the full carat. So don't be obsessed with trying to get closer than .10 point on full-carated stones, but you will find .90's and 1.90's, etc. With half-carat and in-between sizes you will be able to get within .01 point, and find .49's, .69's, 1.49's and so forth.

The one potential problem with buying shy is a psychological one. What sort of person is your True Love? If she's going to be upset that you didn't get the full carat, and will forever think of you as a cheapskate, then it may be worth the extra money.

Your fiancée may never ask how big her 90-point diamond is, but if she does, you might say, "About a carat," and leave it at that. I believe that happiness is a dream that becomes a reality – and if she sees a diamond that is just what she dreamed of, she'll be happy!

Of course, if you're a practical couple and you decide to shop for the diamond together, you should both read this book first and then decide what you're going to shop for.

Fred's Advice: Always buy shy! You'll pay a lot less for a diamond that looks just as good.

❧ Buying Shy Price List ❧

.49 carat

COLOR	IF	VVS1	VVS2	VS1	VS2	SI1	SI2	I1	I2	I3
D	2744	2597	2401	1960	1715	1421	1274	1029	784	637
E	2597	2499	2303	1862	1617	1372	1225	980	784	637
F	2499	2303	2107	1862	1519	1323	1176	931	735	588
G	2205	2009	1862	1568	1470	1274	1127	882	735	588
H	1764	1666	1617	1372	1274	1176	1029	833	686	588
I	1568	1470	1372	1274	1225	1078	980	784	686	588
J	1323	1274	1176	1127	1078	980	931	735	686	539
K	1176	1127	1078	980	931	882	833	686	637	539
L	1078	1029	980	931	882	833	784	637	588	490
M	931	931	882	833	784	735	686	588	539	441

Example: 0.49 carat, I2 (Clarity), G (Color) = $735

Buying Shy Price List

.69 carat

COLOR	IF	VVS1	VVS2	VS1	VS2	SI1	SI2	I1	I2	I3
D	5727	4692	4278	3519	2898	2484	2001	1587	1242	966
E	4692	4347	3726	3312	2829	2415	1932	1518	1173	897
F	4347	3795	3381	3105	2760	2277	1863	1449	1104	897
G	3795	3381	3105	2967	2622	2139	1794	1380	1104	828
H	3243	2967	2691	2553	2277	2070	1725	1311	1035	828
I	2622	2415	2277	2070	1932	1794	1656	1242	1035	828
J	2208	2070	1932	1863	1794	1725	1587	1173	1035	759
K	1794	1725	1656	1587	1518	1449	1311	1104	966	759
L	1725	1656	1587	1518	1449	1380	1242	966	897	690
M	1449	1380	1380	1311	1242	1173	1104	897	828	621

Example: 0.69 carat, SI2 (Clarity), G (Color) = $1,794

.90 carat

COLOR	IF	VVS1	VVS2	VS1	VS2	SI1	SI2	I1	I2	I3
D	8280	6480	6030	5490	4770	4050	3330	2700	2160	1440
E	6570	6030	5490	4860	4320	3870	3330	2700	2070	1350
F	6030	5490	4770	4410	4230	3780	3240	2700	1980	1350
G	5490	4770	4410	4230	4050	3690	3150	2610	1890	1260
H	4770	4410	4230	4050	3870	3600	3060	2520	1890	1260
I	4230	4050	3870	3690	3510	3330	2880	2430	1800	1170
J	3870	3780	3600	3420	3240	3060	2700	2340	1710	1170
K	3330	3240	3150	2970	2790	2700	2340	1980	1620	1080
L	2970	2610	2520	2430	2340	2250	1980	1800	1440	990
M	2250	2160	2160	2070	1980	1890	1800	1710	1350	990

Example: 0.90 carat, VS2 (Clarity), L (Color) = $2,340

❧ Buying Shy Price List ❧

1.49 carat

COLOR	IF	VVS1	VVS2	VS1	VS2	SI1	SI2	I1	I2	I3
D	23840	16539	14304	11622	9685	8493	7599	5513	3874	2682
E	16539	14453	11622	10132	9387	8344	7450	5364	3874	2533
F	14453	11920	10281	9834	9089	8195	7301	5215	3725	2533
G	11771	10430	9685	9238	8642	8046	7152	5066	3576	2384
H	10281	9387	8940	8493	8195	7748	6854	4917	3427	2384
I	9089	8642	8195	7897	7599	7152	6407	4768	3278	2235
J	8344	8046	7748	7450	7152	6556	5960	4470	3129	2235
K	7599	7301	7152	6854	6407	6109	5513	4172	2980	2086
L	6407	6258	6109	5811	5513	5215	4917	3874	2831	1937
M	5364	5215	5066	4768	4619	4172	3874	3278	2682	1937

Example: 1.49 carat, VS1 (Clarity), L (Color) = $9,834

1.90 carat

COLOR	IF	VVS1	VVS2	VS1	VS2	SI1	SI2	I1	I2	I3
D	33250	22990	20900	17480	14250	12160	11020	7790	5510	3610
E	22990	21090	17670	14820	13680	11970	10450	7600	5510	3420
F	21090	18050	15390	14060	13110	11780	10260	7410	5320	3420
G	17860	15390	13870	13300	12350	11400	10070	7220	5130	3230
H	15200	13490	12730	12350	11780	11210	9690	7030	4940	3230
I	12920	12350	11780	11400	10830	10070	9120	6840	4750	3040
J	11970	11590	11020	10830	10260	9500	8550	6460	4560	3040
K	10830	10450	10070	9690	9120	8550	7790	5890	4370	2850
L	9120	8740	8550	8170	7790	7410	6840	5510	4180	2660
M	7600	7410	7220	6840	6460	5890	5510	4750	3800	2660

Example: 1.90 carat, VVS2 (Clarity), J (Color) = $11,020

❧ Buying Shy Price List ❧

2.90 carat

COLOR	IF	VVS1	VVS2	VS1	VS2	SI1	SI2	I1	I2	I3
D	72500	55680	48430	38280	30740	23780	19140	13050	8990	6090
E	55680	48430	38280	33060	27550	23200	18850	12760	8990	5800
F	48430	38570	34220	28420	26390	22620	18560	12470	8990	5510
G	38280	34220	28130	26390	24650	21460	17980	12180	8700	5510
H	32770	27550	25520	24070	21750	19720	17110	11890	8410	5220
I	25230	23780	22910	20590	18850	17690	15950	11600	8120	4930
J	22040	21170	20010	18560	17400	16240	14500	11310	7830	4930
K	18270	17690	17110	16530	15950	14790	13340	10440	7540	4640
L	15370	14790	14210	13630	13050	12470	11600	9570	7250	4350
M	13050	12470	11890	11310	10730	9860	9280	8120	6670	4350

Example: 2.90 carat, SI1 (Clarity), I (Color) = $17,690

3.90 carat

COLOR	IF	VVS1	VVS2	VS1	VS2	SI1	SI2	I1	I2	I3
D	154050	111930	94380	72930	59280	48750	36270	27300	16770	9360
E	111930	96720	73320	59280	52650	45630	37050	27690	16380	8970
F	94380	73710	59670	52650	49140	42510	35490	26130	15600	8580
G	72930	59670	52650	49140	43290	37830	33930	24570	15210	8190
H	59280	52260	47970	43290	37830	32370	31200	23010	14430	8190
I	46410	42510	40560	37440	31980	29250	28860	21840	13650	7800
J	38610	36660	35100	31980	28860	26520	26130	20280	12870	7410
K	34320	32370	30810	28080	25740	23400	22620	17940	12090	7020
L	26910	25740	24570	23400	21450	19110	18330	15210	11310	6630
M	21840	21060	20280	19500	18720	16770	16380	13650	10530	6630

Example: 3.90 carat, VVS1 (Clarity), H (Color) = $52,260

Buying Shy Price List

4.90 carat

COLor	IF	VVS1	VVS2	VS1	VS2	SI1	SI2	I1	I2	I3
D	203350	150430	128380	98980	81830	67620	49000	37240	21070	11760
E	150430	128380	98980	81830	73500	62720	46550	34790	20580	11270
F	128380	99470	82320	72030	67130	57820	44590	32830	19600	10780
G	98980	82320	72520	67130	58310	50470	42630	30870	19110	10290
H	79380	72030	64680	58310	50960	45570	39200	28910	18130	10290
I	62230	57330	53410	50960	47040	40670	36260	27440	17150	9800
J	49980	47530	45080	42630	40180	35770	32830	25480	16170	9310
K	44100	41650	39690	36750	34300	30870	28420	22540	15190	8820
L	35280	33320	32340	30870	28910	25970	23030	19110	14210	8330
M	29400	27930	27400	26460	25480	23030	20580	17150	12230	8330

Example: 4.90 carat, IF (Clarity), D (Color) = $203,350

64

TO THINE OWN SELF BE TRUE:
WHAT KIND OF CUSTOMER ARE YOU?

In my years in the business I've come across five basic kinds of folks who buy diamonds. Tell me what type you are, and I'll recommend what grade of diamond you should buy.

Customer #1 will tell me the three most important things about a diamond are *size, size and size.* The bigger the better, never mind if the stone is yellow and has a few black spots or cracks!

My recommendation:

Weight	1 carat plus
Clarity	I2
Color	L-M

Customer #2 also wants a big diamond, but size isn't the only thing. A little quality wouldn't hurt. Maybe the diamond can be slightly yellow, but please, no obvious cracks or spots. Maybe some teeny spots that can hardly be seen.

My recommendation:

Weight	.50 carat or bigger
Clarity	I1
Color	K

Customer #3 is a balanced kind of person, yin and yang. Size and quality are equal values. The diamond doesn't have to be perfect, but it should be clean to the eye, white and sparkly.

My recommendation:

Weight	.50 carat or bigger
Clarity	SI1
Color	I-J

Customer #4 demands *Quality*, with a capital "Q." Everything else is secondary. The diamond must be not only eye-clean, but clean when viewed with a 10X loupe, and bright white without a *hint* of yellow.

My recommendation:

Weight	.50 carat or bigger
Clarity	VS1
Color	G

Customer #5 isn't getting engaged, or buying an anniversary stone. The diamond is an investment, to be locked away and later resold for a profit.

My recommendation:

Shape	Round (No other!)
Weight	1 carat or bigger
Clarity	VVS1 to Flawless
Color	D, E or F

Diamond Myth

"Diamonds Are a Bad Investment"

Diamonds are probably not a great investment for the average person, but they are not a bad investment for someone who buys wisely and well. Since the diamond crash of 1979, when one carat flawless diamonds fell in value from $75,000 to $15,000, diamond prices have increased steadily. That's largely due to the tightly controlled world diamond market.

Take a look at this chart. Find your type, your budget, and the size diamond you'll be able to afford. This table will help you get the most bang for your buck, whatever type of customer you happen to be.

❧ Buying Guide by Customer Type ❧

Budget	1	2	3	4	5
$250	0.41 carat	0.30 carat	0.25 carat	n/a	n/a
$500	0.50 carat	0.45 carat	0.33 carat	0.29 carat	n/a
$750	0.62 carat	0.50 carat	0.45 carat	0.29 carat	n/a
$1,000	0.75 carat	0.65 carat	0.49 carat	0.38 carat	n/a
$1,250	0.75 carat	0.69 carat	0.50 carat	0.45 carat	n/a
$1,500	0.95 carat	0.75 carat	0.55 carat	0.49 carat	n/a
$1,750	1.00 carat	0.89 carat	0.68 carat	0.49 carat	n/a
$2,000	1.25 carat	0.90 carat	0.69 carat	0.49 carat	n/a
$2,250	1.25 carat	0.99 carat	0.69 carat	0.50 carat	n/a
$2,500	1.49 carat	0.99 carat	0.71 carat	0.58 carat	n/a
$2,700	1.49 carat	1.00 carat	0.80 carat	0.62 carat	n/a
$3,000	1.60 carat	1.15 carat	0.89 carat	0.69 carat	n/a
$3,500	1.75 carat	1.25 carat	0.94 carat	0.75 carat	n/a
$4,000	1.99 carat	1.45 carat	0.99 carat	0.87 carat	n/a
$4,500	2.00 carat	1.50 carat	1.00 carat	0.94 carat	n/a
$5,000	2.20 carat	1.65 carat	1.12 carat	0.99 carat	n/a
$5,500	2.40 carat	1.85 carat	1.25 carat	0.99 carat	n/a
$6,000	2.60 carat	1.99 carat	1.38 carat	1.05 carat	n/a
$7,000	2.99 carat	2.00 carat	1.49 carat	1.15 carat	n/a
$8,000	3.20 carat	2.30 carat	1.59 carat	1.25 carat	1.00 carat
$9,000	3.60 carat	2.66 carat	1.81 carat	1.41 carat	1.14 carat
$10,000	3.99 carat	2.99 carat	1.99 carat	1.56 carat	1.27 carat
$11,000	4.20 carat	2.99 carat	1.99 carat	1.72 carat	1.39 carat

Buying Guide by Customer Type

Budget	1	2	3	4	5
$12,000	4.60 carat	2.99 carat	2.00 carat	1.87 carat	1.49 carat
$13,000	4.99 carat	3.00 carat	2.16 carat	1.99 carat	1.49 carat
$14,500	5.00 carat	3.25 carat	2.41 carat	1.99 carat	1.50 carat
$15,000	5.00 carat	3.50 carat	2.50 carat	1.99 carat	1.61 carat
$15,500	5.34 carat	3.60 carat	2.58 carat	1.99 carat	1.66 carat
$16,000	5.51 carat	3.72 carat	2.66 carat	1.99 carat	1.72 carat
$16,500	5.69 carat	3.84 carat	2.75 carat	1.99 carat	1.77 carat
$17,000	5.86 carat	3.95 carat	2.83 carat	1.99 carat	1.83 carat
$17,500	5.99 carat	3.99 carat	2.92 carat	1.99 carat	1.88 carat
$18,000	6.15 carat	4.00 carat	2.99 carat	2.04 carat	1.94 carat
$18,500	6.32 carat	4.11 carat	2.99 carat	2.10 carat	1.99 carat
$19,000	6.47 carat	4.22 carat	2.99 carat	2.16 carat	1.99 carat
$19,500	6.65 carat	4.33 carat	2.99 carat	2.22 carat	1.99 carat
$20,000	6.82 carat	4.44 carat	2.99 carat	2.27 carat	1.99 carat
$25,000	7.00 carat	5.00 carat	3.00 carat	2.84 carat	1.99 carat
$30,000	8.00 carat	5.88 carat	3.99 carat	2.99 carat	2.24 carat
$35,000	9.00 carat	6.86 carat	4.21 carat	2.99 carat	2.61 carat
$40,000	10.00 carat	7.55 carat	4.82 carat	3.17 carat	2.99 carat
$45,000	n/a	8.37 carat	4.99 carat	3.57 carat	2.99 carat
$50,000	n/a	8.99 carat	5.00 carat	3.97 carat	2.99 carat
$55,000	n/a	9.76 carat	5.50 carat	3.99 carat	2.99 carat
$60,000	n/a	9.99 carat	5.99 carat	4.35 carat	3.18 carat
$70,000	n/a	10.00 carat	6.93 carat	4.99 carat	3.70 carat
$80,000	n/a	n/a	7.40 carat	4.99 carat	3.99 carat
$90,000	n/a	n/a	8.18 carat	4.99 carat	4.43 carat
$100,000	n/a	n/a	8.99 carat	5.46 carat	4.93 carat

CHAPTER THREE

RING SETTINGS

O NCE you have decided on a diamond, you'll need to select a setting. I mean, diamonds are beautiful, but what good are they unless you can wear them?

There are three basic types of ring settings: The Tiffany Setting, Bridal Sets, and Diamond Wedding Rings.

Tiffany

The Tiffany Setting, named after the famed jeweler Louis C. Tiffany, is a simple, elegant setting that lets the diamond be the star of the show and be in the spotlight. In a Tiffany Setting, the stone is held by four to six prongs, depending on the shape of the diamond.

Note: *When buying a ring that uses prongs to hold the diamond, make sure the prongs are white gold or platinum. Yellow gold prongs will give the stone a yellow cast.*

Three basic styles of settings: Bridal Set (far left), the Tiffany (middle), and Diamond Wedding Ring (right).

Bridal Sets

The bridal set is a perennial favorite. It consists of an engagement ring and a wedding band made to fit together to look like one ring.

Diamond Wedding Rings

The diamond wedding ring is large enough to be worn by itself, and can serve as the engagement ring and the wedding ring all in one. In many of these settings there is a main diamond surrounded by several smaller stones.

ACCENTS: BAGUETTES, MELEE, TRILLIANTS

These are small diamonds that are set around the main stone.

Baguettes are small, elongated diamonds, usually under .15 carats in weight, either tapered or nontapered. Melee are round diamonds, under .20 carat. Trilliants are triangular in shape, usually under .33 carat.

Baguettes under .15 carat cost approximately $1,400 per carat. Trilliants under .33 carat cost approximately $1,500 per carat. Melee under .20 carat cost around $950 per carat. (Wholesale prices, based on SI1-H or I color grade.)

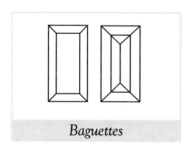

Baguettes

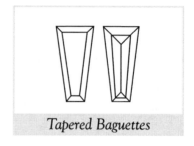

Tapered Baguettes

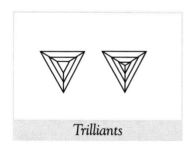

Trilliants

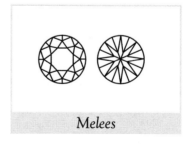

Melees

ADDING COLOR

Of course diamonds are a girl's best friend, but rubies, sapphires, emeralds and other colored stones are pretty good pals, too! Many women like to surround their diamonds with colored gems, or vice-versa, and your True Love might like her diamond accented with her birthstone. There are some stunning combinations of diamonds and other precious stones. Ask your jeweler to show you some.

A WORD ABOUT GOLD...

Most engagement rings and wedding bands are made of gold. Pure gold is stamped 24K (24 Karat), which means it has not been mixed with any other metals. We don't use 24K gold for jewelry because it's too soft, and will bend too easily.

> 18K gold is 75% pure gold. Other metals such as copper, zinc or nickel have been added for strength.
>
> 14K gold is 58.5% pure gold, and 41.5% other metals for strength.
>
> 10K gold is mostly other metals and should not be considered for jewelry.

You might see gold jewelry stamped with a number – 750 or 585. This is the European system of grading gold. 1000 is pure gold, or 24K; 750 is 75% pure gold, or 18K; 585 is 58.5% pure gold, or 14K.

Gold "Allergy"

Some women, after wearing gold jewelry for awhile, will find that it leaves a black mark or smudge on their skin. This is caused by perspiration reacting with the metals mixed with the gold, and not from a "gold allergy." Usually a switch from 14K to 18K gold will solve the problem. But if you are the one-in-a-million who still reacts to 18K, switch to platinum. Your body has expensive tastes!

...AND PLATINUM

Platinum is a rarer metal than gold, and somewhat harder for a jeweler to work with. As you might guess, this makes it more expensive than gold. It is stronger than gold and therefore holds the diamond more securely — and some women prefer platinum because they feel it shows off the diamond better than gold.

How Do I Get My True Love's Ring Size?

The simplest way, of course, is to ask her. The only problem with this method is that it might tip her off that you're going to propose. For many suitors, that would be a disaster — statistics show that seven out of ten men shop alone and plan to surprise their intended. The other three take the low-risk route — they propose first, then shop for a diamond with the lady. If you're in the latter group, you can check her ring size at the jeweler's.

Another way is to get your hands on a ring she has worn on her third finger, left hand. Take it to a jeweler, who can quickly tell you the ring size. Don't forget to return the ring promptly!

A third way is to ask her mother. This might be even scarier than proposing, but going to her mom first can be a great idea. It can often tell you three key things: One, your beloved's ring size. Two, how the parents feel about you as a potential son-in-law. And, three, the mom can give you a pretty good reading on how your proposal will be received. This way you'll be a lot more sure of the outcome before making this expensive purchase.

CHAPTER FOUR

PICKING THE

JEWELER

NOW that you know what you're looking for, and how to look, the next step is to determine where to shop for your diamond. Before you visit every jeweler in the area, "let your fingers do the walking." You'll find lots of jewelers in the Yellow Pages, under "Jewelers, Retail," and also under "Diamonds." Many merchants advertise in both places. You'll see a variety of information in the advertisements. Some will only mention their "lowest prices." Others will note that the jeweler is a "Graduate Gemologist," or that they sell "GIA Certified" diamonds. To narrow down your search, limit it to jewelers who advertise their GIA and Gemologist credentials.

Using the following questionnaire sheet, spend an hour on the phone calling jewelers and screening them to make sure they have the qualifications you're after. Add up the scores, and visit the top three on your Scoreboard.

Jeweler Questionnaire Sheet (J.Q.S.): A Worksheet

Enter the points earned for each answer.

Score

_____1. How do their prices compare to the wholesale prices listed in this book?

At wholesale	(50 pts)
10% over wholesale	(25 pts)
50% over wholesale	(10 pts)
Double wholesale	(-10 pts)

_____2. Can they supply an "FTC Regulated Lab" certificate with the diamond?

Yes	(10 pts)
No	(0 pts)

_____3. Can they provide a GIA appraisal with the diamond?

Yes	(10 pts)
No	(0 pts)

78

_____4. Do they have a gem laboratory where the stone
can be viewed?

Yes   (10 pts)
No   (0 pts)

_____5. Do they have a master set of diamonds for color grading?

Yes   (10 pts)
No   (0 pts)

_____6. Do they have a gem diamond light for color grading?

Yes   (10 pts)
No   (0 pts)

_____7. Do they have an ultraviolet light for color grading?

Yes   (10 pts)
No   (0 pts)

_____8. Do they have a 10X 20.5mm triplet loupe?

10X 20.5 triplet   (15 pts)
Any 10X loupe   (10 pts)

_____9.   Do they have a gem scope or microscope to
          view diamonds?

          Yes   (10 pts)
          No   (0 pts)

_____10. Do they use the GIA grading scale for color
          and clarity?

          If they use the GIA scale   (15 pts)
          An automatic disqualification if they do not.

_____11. Are the diamonds loose (not mounted)?

          If the answer is yes   (15 pts)
          If the answer is no, this is an automatic disqualification!

_____12. Do they have an electronic scale to weigh
          the diamonds?

          If the answer is yes   (15 pts)
          If the answer is no, this is an automatic disqualification!

_____13. Do they custom-cut diamonds to order?

Yes   (10 pts)
No   (0 pts)

_____14. Do they make their own jewelry on the premises?

Yes   (10 pts)
No   (0 pts)

_____15. How large is their loose diamond inventory?

$250,000 and over   (15 pts)
Under $250,000   (0 pts)

_____16. Do they own the inventory, or are they dealing in memorandum diamonds?

If they have their own inventory (25 pts)

_____17. What is their trade-in policy?

Equal to what you pay for the diamond   (20 pts)
Less than what you pay for the diamond   (0 pts)
No trade-in policy   (-25 pts)

_____18. Do they have a return policy?

   If they have a 30, 60 or 90-day unconditional
   return policy   (20 pts)
   For a return policy based on possible
   misrepresentation that is, if you find that the stone
   isn't exactly what the jeweler said it was. (15 pts)
   Automatic disqualification for no return policy.

_____19. Does the store specialize in diamonds (or do they also
   sell watches, gold chains, etc.)?

   Yes   (10 pts)
   No   (0 pts)

_____20. Where is the store located?

   If the store is in an office building, such as Boston's
   Jewelers' Building   (10 pts)
   If the store has an ordinary street address (0 pts)
   If the store is in a mall   (-10 pts)

_____21. How long has the store been around?

   More than two years   (10 pts)
   Less than two years   (0 pts)

_____22. Is the jeweler American Gem Society (AGS) rated?
Yes   (10 pts)
No   (0 pts)

_____23. Do they have a GIA gemologist on staff?
Yes   (10 pts)
Automatic disqualification if they do not.

_____24. Do they see customers by appointment only?
Yes   (10 pts)
No   (0 pts)

_____ *Total Score*   ❧ | Rating | ☙

375-425 points = Superior
325-374 points = Acceptable
275-324 points = Marginal
Below 275: Keep looking!

❧ | Jeweler's Scores | ☙

#1_____   _____

#2_____   _____

#3_____   _____

THE GIFT OF JEWELRY

The engagement ring may be the first piece of fine jewelry you buy, but chances are, it won't be the last. A gift of fine jewelry is appropriate at any season of the year and in any season of life. Birthdays, anniversaries, Christmas, Chanukah, the first day of spring, Mother's Day, Valentine's Day — jewelry is always an excellent gift.

You should take as much care buying a birthday gift as you do when you shop for an engagement ring, to make sure you get the most value for your loved one and your budget. Whether it's a diamond or some other precious stone, many of the same rules apply. And always keep the recipient uppermost in your mind. Use the Gift Questionnaire Sheet below. It'll help you match the gift to the person, and ensure that the gift will be happily received and worn with pride.

GIFT QUESTIONNAIRE SHEET: A WORKSHEET

Here are some things to think about before making an expensive jewelry purchase, whether it's an engagement ring, a birthday gift, or a gift for some other special occasion. You may already know all or most of this information, but you probably haven't thought about it in terms of buying a ring. Take the time to fill out this questionnaire, and you're almost guaranteed to be on target with your purchase.

1. Birth date: _____

   The birth date tells you the birthstone (see page 152). Sometimes women like their engagement ring or wedding band to have their birthstone mixed with diamonds. Or, a birthstone ring is a nice gift by itself.

2. Height & Weight: _____

   You can guess at these if you have to. Sometimes these vital stats will help you make an educated guess of someone's ring size, if you don't know it. It also helps you get a ring that's in proportion with body type. For example, a half-carat diamond may look fine on a person of average build, but might look small on a larger person.

3. Favorite color: _____

This is important information! If your True Love's favorite color is blue, a diamond set with sapphire accent stones might be perfect. In some cases, the color might be so important she'll want the colored stone as the main stone.

4. Personality type:

( ) Conservative ( ) Traditional ( ) Flamboyant

( ) Contemporary ( ) Trendsetter

The choice of settings is virtually unlimited. The personality type will narrow down the search. For example, if the person is conservative and very traditional, a diamond solitaire in a Tiffany setting might be perfect.

5. Ring size: _____

Very important. The last thing we want to do is take the ring back to have it sized. (See page 76).

6. Profession: _____

Some professionals can't wear jewelry to work, or must wear modest jewelry. A ring might actually interfere with some jobs, so the person should be able to remove it easily. In some professions (real estate broker, stockbroker, model) a "knock-out" ring is an indicator of success.

7. Diamond shape: _____

Ask if you must, but find out what her favorite diamond shape is. Personality type can be an indicator — the traditionalist would probably favor a round stone (65% of all engagement rings have round stones) while a trendsetter may like a fancy shape. After round, the most popular shapes are marquise, pear, oval, emerald cut, radiant, quadrillion, and heart. Don't buy her a heart-shaped diamond unless she specifically asks for it — it's probably the least attractive.

8. Carat size: _____

Ask a woman what size diamond she wants, and she's likely to ask, "How big can I get?" The best way to go about this is to determine your budget and check the price guides in this book.

Size Scale:

Average:	.38 points
Yuppie:	Around one carat
Ultimate Dream:	Two to three carats
Filthy Rich:	Three to five carats

Is the recipient *size* conscious or *quality* conscious? You'll need to have some idea, to know whether you can trade off a little quality for a bigger carat size or vice-versa.

9. Setting color:

    ( ) Yellow gold   ( ) White gold   ( ) Platinum

    Nine out of ten women like yellow gold, but it's important
    to be sure. Look at her other jewelry. (Don't forget, on a
    yellow gold ring make sure the prongs are white gold or
    platinum so they don't make the diamond appear yellow.)

10. Purity: ( ) 10K   ( ) 14K   ( ) 18K   ( ) 22K

    Most jewelry worn by most women is 14K. 18K is a little
    softer and a little yellower. Platinum is white. Unless she
    specifies 18K or platinum, 14K is a safe choice.

11. Other favorite jewelry: _____

    You might want to match the color or style of other
    favorite pieces of jewelry.

12. Is there a particular ring she has admired?

    Pay attention to your True Love and you'll learn a lot
    about likes and dislikes, and you may hear her admire
    someone else's ring, or a picture of a ring in a magazine. If
    you're lucky she may even say, "That's exactly the kind of
    ring I'd love to have."

THE NEW YORK DIAMOND DISTRICT

"Bargains Galore" or "Buyer Beware"?

The fabled New York Diamond District, centered on 47th Street in Manhattan, probably has more diamond dealers per square foot than any place on earth. For a couple of bustling blocks, the streets are teeming with diamond sellers, practically hawking their wares as if they were selling hot pretzels. The diamond trade here is dominated by hastening figures who lend the place an unmatched mystique as they shuttle between cutting houses and shops, carrying hundreds of thousands of dollars worth of diamonds in their pockets and satchels. But is this a good place to buy a diamond?

In my experience, it is probably the most difficult place in America to get a good deal on a good diamond. You have a better chance of winning the lottery or getting hit by lightning than getting a good diamond deal on 47th Street!

The whole place is attitude and hustle. They employ a kind of reverse psychology — here, the dealer doesn't trust the customer! The dealers give you the impression they haven't really got the time or the inclination to deal with you. "You really want a diamond? Okay, hurry up and pick something out, pay me and please leave. I have more important things to do than sell you one measly diamond. Certificates? Guarantees? Whaddya want, papers or diamonds? You want to buy — here, take it. You don't want to buy — try the guy down the street, maybe he has time to deal with papers, I deal with diamonds!"

I bought a diamond on 47th Street one day. Dressed in a business suit, I went shopping, settled on a dealer, and asked for a one-carat, VS1-G. I was given a stone that was said to fit my specs. When I asked for paperwork, the dealer gave me something that fudged on the grades, that said the stone was "VS," but not VS1, and "G-H," not G. Two days later, dressed in jeans, I returned to the same dealer. He didn't recognize me. When I showed him the stone and told him what I'd paid for it, he immediately started berating me: "You got taken! You paid too much for this diamond! You should have come to me in the first place!" When I pulled out my receipt and reminded him I'd bought the stone from him two days ago, he practically pushed me out of the store.

Everyone in New York "knows a guy on 47th Street" who will allegedly give you the diamond deal of a lifetime if you mention the right name. Friends, it ain't that easy.

I've found that if you get above street level on 47th Street, up to the dealers on the higher floors, you can get a decent deal on a diamond if you're a shrewd buyer. Even up there, above the hustle and bustle, dealers pressure you to move quickly on a purchase. Take your time. Examine the stone closely, go through all the steps I outline in this book, *pay by credit card (never cash!)* and get an independent appraisal immediately.

90

Every major city has its diamond center, and some of them are excellent places to purchase diamonds if you shop for the right dealer and ask the right questions. But the New York Diamond District? Toughest place I know to buy a diamond.

 Inside the Diamond Business

A few years ago, an industry group conducted a national survey to see how honestly diamond dealers were doing business with the public. The bottom line: not very.

The group sent diamond experts posing as ordinary customers into jewelry stores across the country. The experts found that the *average* dealer gave his diamonds a "two-grade bump." That is, they sold their diamonds *two grades higher than they actually were*. For example, if a GIA gemologist rated a stone's clarity and color as SI1-J, the jeweler would tell you it was a VS1-H — two grades higher, and a lot more expensive. The investigators quietly told jewelers to clean up their act.

But is this stuff still going on? You bet it is! The "bumps" are almost always in clarity and color, because those are the hardest things for the average customer to judge. Beware, and be doubtful of the jeweler's grading. Compare color against a master set, and look carefully at the stone with a 10X loupe for inclusions and blemishes that can affect clarity.

Buying Diamonds on the Internet

In this age of the "Information Superhighway," many people are connecting to the Internet for a wide variety of reasons, including home shopping. You can sit at your computer terminal, browse the World Wide Web, and find thousands of items for sale — including diamonds! That's right, companies are selling diamonds over the Internet.

Here's how it works. You locate a diamond merchant on the Web, and look over a selection of stones. Full-color, high-resolution images of the diamonds are displayed on your screen. The diamonds are graded by carat weight, cut, clarity and color. You select a stone you like, enter your American Express or Visa number, and your diamond will be shipped. It's refundable, of course, if you decide not to keep the stone.

Sounds great, doesn't it? Shopping for diamonds from the comfort of your home! Well, I tried it myself — and I was not impressed. Here's what I found. I shopped through the selections of five dealers, choosing 20 diamonds that looked good on my computer screen and seemed to have the qualities I was looking for in terms of cut, clarity and color. And what do you suppose happened?

Out of the 20 diamonds I selected on my Internet shopping trip — *I found no winners*.

Seventeen of the diamonds I chose were poorly cut. The other three were "not available." twenty strikeouts in twenty at-bats! Not a very good average in any league.

Some of the Internet marketing practices I found:

- They offer lots of full-carated diamonds (1ct, 1.5ct, 2ct, 2.5 ct, etc.) and very few opportunities to "buy shy" (see page 58). They try to force the buyer to their strong suit where their inventories are heaviest. Tell them what you want, and stick to it — don't settle for what they say they have. If you want a .90 SI1-I, then don't let a salesman push you into a 1ct SI1-G. (If he says he'll give you the 1ct SI1-G at the .90 SI1-I price, that's okay!)

- Lots of "off-makes" (poorly proportioned stones). I could tell they were taking rough which, if properly cut, would have yielded shy-carated stones, and cutting them heavy to reach full-carat weights even if it meant sacrificing sparkle for size.

- One dealer actually marked spread-cut diamonds with a "+" sign, offering them as more desirable (and more expensive), claiming they were more brilliant and looked "larger than would be expected" for their weight. Well, we know that a spread-cut diamond offers brilliance at the expense of fire, and probably has a thin girdle which would cause a durability problem.

93

- I found more "bait and switch" tactics than in regular diamond markets.

- They offered GIA certificates with their diamonds, but the certificates were old. Never accept a certificate older than six months! You never know where that diamond has been or what's been done to it since it was certified. If they're convinced their old diamond is so wonderful, have them re-certify it free.

My bottom line on Internet diamond shopping is, if you know what you're doing and you have time and patience, you can find good diamonds on the Internet and save an average of 20-25% off normal retail. But they've stacked the deck against you — they've got a ton of losers, and only a few winners which they show on the screen. You're forced to hunt for the needle in the haystack. If you follow my guidelines and do your homework, the Internet is a viable option for getting a great diamond, BUT, with the same hard work you can get the same (or better) deal at your local jewelry store. And wouldn't you rather see what you're getting before you put your money down?

DIAMONDS BY MAIL

You can buy diamonds through the mail, but this greatly restricts your ability to shop effectively. If you plan to purchase a diamond through the mail, here's a checklist:

- Make sure the firm has been in business for at least two years.

- *Only* buy with a credit card! That way you can return the diamond for a full refund if you're not happy with it.

- Ask if they will provide bank viewing of the diamond. The seller sends the diamond to a bank. The bank guarantees the security of the stone. You view the diamond at the bank with an appraiser. If you decide to buy, you pay the bank and the bank pays the seller. This arrangement provides security for both parties.

- If you're not going the bank viewing route, make sure they have a return policy.

- Ask if they will provide certification by an FTC-approved laboratory.

- Find out if mounting is available. Otherwise, you'll have to take the stone to a jeweler, where you probably should have gone in the first place!

TO CERTIFY OR NOT TO CERTIFY?

People are always asking me how important it is to get a lab certificate when they buy diamonds. The simple answer is: *it's not.*

We've seen how just the *threat* or suggestion of certification is enough to keep most jewelers relatively honest. The only times I feel that a certificate is essential are:

1. You are a diamond investor buying investment-grade diamonds (Flawless, Internally Flawless, VVS1 or VVS2 D, E and F color grades).

2. You are a diamond investor buying a fancy colored diamond and you need certification that the color origin of the diamond is natural.

Some readers of this book may have misinterpreted my advice about certification, and think that a diamond is worthless unless it comes with a lab certificate. *Not true!* Typically, only investment-grade diamonds have certification. It would be impractical, costly and unnecessary for jewelers to certify every stone they sell.

When you're diamond shopping, ask the jeweler if the stone you're interested in has a lab certificate. If it doesn't, ask if he would mind certifying it. If the response is, "Sure, no problem, I'll get that for you within ten days at no cost," you can be pretty sure it's not necessary. But if the dealer tries to weasel out of it, and gives you excuses about long delays and extra fees, you can be pretty sure that dealer isn't being honest about diamond grades.

"Fake" Diamonds

Many customers want to be reassured that their diamond is really a diamond. This should not be a major worry, unless you bought your diamond from a guy on the street. No legitimate jeweler, even one who might try to cheat on color and clarity grades, is going to slip you a piece of glass, a cubic zirconia or even a synthetic diamond and try to pass it off as a real diamond.

Diamond Substitutes

Cubic Zirconia (CZ)

A CZ is not a "man-made diamond." It's a diamond simulant that looks similar to a diamond. It does not have any of the properties of a diamond — it simply looks like a diamond. And while a well-made CZ looks pretty darned good, it doesn't have anywhere near the hardness of a diamond and will quickly become worn and dull. Any good jeweler can spot the difference between a diamond and a CZ in a moment. I think the CZ has a plastic look, and has a light blue cast through the entire stone. The sure way to tell is to weigh the stone — a CZ will weigh 75% more than a diamond of the same size!

Synthetic Diamonds

A synthetic diamond is a man-made diamond. It's pure carbon subjected to intense heat and pressure — same as a natural diamond. But it's not a natural diamond, and a gemologist can tell the difference. Synthetics do not appreciate in value and have no trade-in value. In April 1995, synthetic diamonds became available to the public, selling for about two-thirds the cost of natural diamonds. There is no secondary market for these stones, so if you buy one you're stuck with it forever. If you tried to resell it you'd get back only 10% of your initial investment, versus an 80% resell average for a good quality natural diamond that was correctly purchased.

If you are doing long-distance diamond trading, and the buyer isn't able to see the stone before purchase, a certificate can be crucial.

Remember: A certificate must be recent (within six months) and the diamond must not have been worn since certification.

If a jeweler shows you a certificate for a stone, and the certification was done five years ago, it's meaningless! The diamond could have been anywhere and undergone many changes since then.

The best thing to do is find a jeweler who will give you an open-ended certification policy — that is, he will certify the diamond for you, free, at any time in the future. This way, if you need to resell the diamond you can certify it.

Fred's Advice: Only certify a diamond just before resale to guarantee its current quality. Once it is certified, do not allow it to be worn, or it could void the certificate.

The Yehuda Diamond

The Yehuda diamond, relatively new to the diamond marketplace, is named for Zui Yehuda of Israel. He's the man who developed the process of "filling" a flawed diamond to make it more attractive.

Here's how it works. Yehuda takes a diamond that has cracks on the outside and fills the cracks with clear molten glass. The cracks disappear. Using this process, Yehuda can take a stone with an I1 clarity grade and make it look like an SI2. The advantage of the Yehuda diamond is that you can get a slightly better looking diamond without paying a higher price.

The disadvantages of the Yehuda diamond:

- We don't know how long the treatment will last. You might be wearing the diamond one day and it will look great, and the next day the filler will fall out, leaving you with a flawed stone.
- Any repair work on the setting could damage the filler.
- Most people don't like the idea of having a diamond that's not all diamond. If you buy a Yehuda diamond, you might have a very hard time reselling it.

The Federal Trade Commission requires a jeweler to disclose whether a diamond has been treated. But many jewelers don't have the expertise to know if a stone has been treated, and may buy or sell a Yehuda diamond unknowingly.

FTC-Regulated Laboratories in the U.S.

Throughout this book I refer to the Gemological Institute of America (GIA) as the diamond certification authority, simply because they were the first organization in the U.S. to provide lab certificates for diamonds. There are actually three certification centers in the U.S., all regulated by the Federal Trade Commission, and all of equal value.

Gemological Institute of America
1660 Stewart
Santa Monica, CA 90404-4020
1-800-421-7250
   or
580 5th Avenue, Suite 200
New York, NY 10036-4794
(212) 221-5858

European Gemological Laboratory, Inc.
550 South Hill Street, Suite #1595
Los Angeles, CA 90013-2414
1-800-235-3287

International Gemological Institute
579 5th Avenue, 7th Floor
New York, NY 10017
(212) 398-1700

MAKING THE PURCHASE

A Final Review

1. Fill out the Gift Questionnaire Sheet (see page 85).

2. Call all potential jeweler candidates on the phone and have them answer questions on the Jeweler Questionnaire Sheet (see page 78)

3. After you've called all the jewelry stores that you're planning to compare and filled out a Jeweler Questionnaire Sheet on each one, pick the top three rated stores.

4. If for any reason you cannot find a jeweler in your area that satisfies all the requirements, you can call my HelpLine for assistance (see page 179).

5. Before you visit your jeweler choices, call each one and make an appointment. By making an appointment you can be assured that you will get their undivided attention.

6. Once in the jewelry store, look at the diamonds they have to offer. Write down the clarity and color grade of each stone you like and fill out the Proportion Questionnaire Sheet (see page 43) on each stone. Only consider purchasing diamonds that match the carat weight, clarity and color you like and pass the Proportion Questionnaire Sheet. Their prices should also be close to the recommended prices listed in this book.

CHAPTER FIVE

TRICKS OF THE TRADE

BLUE DIAMOND BLUES

Some jewelers may try to market a "blue-white" diamond as though it were a white diamond with a hint of blue, and more valuable than a plain white diamond. It's not! It's a diamond that fluoresces blue and is therefore less valuable. Avoid it!

THE "50% OFF" SALE

Browsing through your Sunday paper you spot an exciting ad: a local jeweler is having a "50% Off" sale on diamonds! Wow! You jump into your car, drive to the store, and you make what you are sure is an incredible buy on a one-carat diamond.

You're still patting yourself on the back a week later when you happen to walk past another jewelry store where you see the same size, same quality diamond selling for less than what you paid — *and it's their regular price!* What happened?

You were taken in by a fake sale. Many jewelers run these sales. They'll take a diamond that is worth, say, $1,000 wholesale and instead of marking it up 100%, which is standard practice, they'll mark it up 400% and tell you that $4,000 is the regular price — when in fact the regular price for such a stone would be $2,000. Then the jeweler takes 50% off the inflated price and sells it to you for full retail, $2,000.

The way to know if you're really getting a sale price is to compare the jeweler's price with the wholesale price list in this book. If the jeweler's regular price is more than double the wholesale price, you're not getting any bargain.

For example: Joe's Jewelry Store has a one-carat VS1-G on sale for $12,400, marked down from $24,800. You look at my price list and see that a one-carat VS1-G wholesales for $6,200. Therefore, full retail should be $12,400. Joe has artificially inflated the "regular" price to trick you into believing you're getting a bargain.

"Bait and Switch"

This is a term that's been around for a long time, and it's not limited to the diamond business. Bait and switch refers to anyone who runs an advertising special on a particular item just to get you into the store. When you go to the store, however, you're told that the advertised item is sold out. Then they try to sell you something else — invariably, something more expensive. The jeweler hopes that since you've already made the trip to the store, you won't want to go home empty-handed.

Don't be impatient! Many people arrive at the store determined to buy something and get talked into something they don't really want. Take control! Grade the jeweler using your Jeweler Questionnaire Sheet, and if he or she passes that test, stick around and look at some diamonds, using a scratch sheet to check each one. Compare the prices to the wholesale prices in this book, to see what kind of deal you're being offered. And for an exact updated price on a particular stone, call my HelpLine.

"IS WHITE REALLY WHITE?"

Jewelers love diamonds that fluoresce blue, and will sometimes install special lighting to enhance the fluorescence of their diamonds. The blue masks the yellow color that might be in the diamond and make it appear to be a higher color grade than it really is. Always take the loose diamond you're looking at and place it on a white background to check the color, and make sure there are no spotlights shining on it. Always ask the jeweler if the stone has fluorescence. If he says no, ask him to prove it by placing it under an ultraviolet lamp so you can see if it glows a particular color. If you decide to buy the diamond, get it in writing whether or not the stone has fluorescence.

"GRADE BUMPING"

The Federal Trade Commission requires that a diamond be within one clarity and color grade of what it is originally sold as. Because of this, jewelers tend to "bump" the grade. For example, if a jeweler buys a stone as a VS1-G, he'll bump it up and sell it as a VVS2-F. If you buy it as a VVS2-F and have it appraised as a VS1-G, the dealer is legally covered, because he sold it within one grade of what it really is.

Fred's Advice: Always ask if the diamond is GIA certified. If it isn't, insist that the sale is contingent on the stone being certified. The jeweler probably won't try to bump the color and clarity if he thinks the stone is going to be checked before you put your money down. Just the threat of GIA certification should be enough – you probably don't have to send it to GIA.

"THE FRACTION SCAM"

Some jewelers will list the weights of their diamonds only in fractions, such as 3/4 of a carat. Your next question should be, "Well, is it 75 points or not?" Many jewelers will call anything from 65 to 75 points a 3/4 carat diamond. These same jewelers will call anything from 90 points to 100 points a full carat. *This is illegal.* A diamond must weigh within *half a point* of its stated weight. You'll notice a jeweler will never round a diamond down — they'd never call an 85-pointer a 3/4 carat stone. Ask the jeweler to weigh the stone, in front of you, on an electronic scale. If he says he can't because it's in a setting, you shouldn't be looking at it anyway. Only buy loose diamonds.

"THE OLD SWITCHEROO"

You've shopped around, rated the jewelers, graded the diamonds, and finally found the stone you want. You lay your money down and order a setting. When you get the ring, you have it independently appraised — only to discover that the diamond in the ring isn't the same stone you purchased! The jeweler has pulled a switcheroo. You go back and confront him, and he accuses *you* of switching stones. What now?

Well, sad to say, you're stuck. There's really nothing you can do, no way to prove a switch was made. You must prevent the switcheroo before it happens.

When you decide on a diamond, get the jeweler to put in writing the exact weight, and the clarity and color grades of the stone. Before the diamond is mounted, have the jeweler show you where the blemishes and inclusions are, and plot them on a drawing. Keep this drawing with you, and when you return to pick up the mounted diamond, check it again, looking for the same flaws that are on your drawing. If they match, you have the right diamond.

"THE SANDBAGGER"

If you've purchased a diamond by following all my instructions, you shouldn't feel the need to go to an independent appraiser to double-check your purchase. But if you do, watch out for the sandbagger! The sandbagger is someone who lies to you and tells you that you've been taken, that your diamond isn't worth what you paid for it. Why would he do that? So that he can recommend where you should buy your diamonds — no doubt at a place which gives him a kickback! Or he may tell you, "You should have bought from me."

Fred's Advice: If you ever want to have the diamond checked, don't take a chance. Send it to the GIA for an unbiased opinion.

"THE VANISHING ACT"

Now you see it — now you don't! Carbon, that is. There is a laser beam process for removing carbon from inside a diamond. It's called *laser drilling*. A diamond that contains black carbon, visible with a 10X loupe, is zapped with a fine laser beam which vaporizes the carbon, removing the black spot.

The problem is that the laser beam creates a *tunnel* from the surface of the diamond to where the carbon used to be. You might not be able to see this tunnel with the naked eye, but you'll see it under a loupe. And if a stone has been drilled several times, it can be weakened.

Laser drilling can make a diamond more attractive to the eye, but it can also lower the resale value. The Federal Trade Commission requires jewelers to disclose to consumers whether a diamond has been laser drilled.

COMMON MYTHS ABOUT DIAMONDS

1. A DIAMOND IS FOREVER

A diamond will only be forever if you take care of it. If you don't a diamond can chip, fracture, or break. Even a diamond should come with a care instruction tag.

2. DIAMONDS ARE VERY RARE

Nope! There is more of a man-made shortage than a natural shortage. The distribution of the number of diamonds put on the market each year is highly regulated. There are really enough diamonds to give each man, woman and child in the United States a whole cupful.

3. WOMEN ARE MORE SIZE CONSCIOUS THAN QUALITY CONSCIOUS

This one is almost true, but not quite. Even though most women believe that bigger is better, there are still quite a few women out there that will sacrifice size to get a better quality diamond.

4. A DIAMOND IS THE MOST EXPENSIVE GEMSTONE

The truth is there are quite a few more expensive gemstones on the market. For example, a top quality ruby can be worth over thirty thousand dollars a carat.

5. A LARGE DIAMOND IS ALWAYS WORTH MORE THAN A SMALL DIAMOND

Size is only one criterion by which a diamond can be judged. A small, high-clarity, high-color diamond can cost more than a large, low-clarity, low-color diamond.

6. AFTER A DIAMOND HAS BEEN CUT, LITTLE DIAMONDS CAN BE CUT FROM THE SHAVINGS

Usually there are no shavings, only dust. Most diamonds are ground down and there aren't any little pieces left over to cut anything else. Most people believe a diamond is whittled, not ground down. This is another myth.

7. A FANCY SHAPED DIAMOND IS MORE DIFFICULT TO CUT THAN A ROUND DIAMOND

All diamonds, to a certain degree, are difficult to cut, and some very large diamonds take more time and effort to cut than smaller diamonds do. But one diamond is not harder to cut than another just because of the shape.

8. DIAMONDS ARE A GOOD INVESTMENT

Webster's dictionary defines investment as "an outlay of money for income or profit." Since most people purchase diamonds to be worn and not to be resold, diamonds are not a good investment. Only through proper education and training could diamonds become a good investment. For the average Joe, I would recommend buying a diamond for the enjoyment and prestige it brings and don't be too concerned about making a buck.

9. A DIAMOND SHOULD BE BOUGHT STRICTLY ON ITS VISUAL APPEARANCE: "IF IT LOOKS GOOD, BUY IT"

A lot of people believe "what I can't see can't hurt me!" Well, we all know that blind ignorance will only lead to disaster. Practically any diamond looks good in a jewelry store. The jeweler spends quite a bit on spotlights to make any quality diamond sparkle. But unless you plan on carrying a spotlight with you everywhere you go, you'd better check the four C's or you might purchase a diamond that only looks good in a jewelry store and is lifeless everywhere else.

10. AN EMERALD CUT DIAMOND IS THE MOST EXPENSIVE SHAPE DIAMOND

I don't know why some people believe this. I constantly have clients tell me that they like emerald cut diamonds but know that they are the most expensive and can't afford them. This is crazy! The emerald cut diamond is the *least* expensive of all the shapes. You see, it is the shape that is most like the natural shape of the rough, so there is a little bit less waste during the cutting process. If you like emerald cut diamonds, enjoy them, don't avoid them; they are not any more expensive.

11. DIAMONDS ARE A BAD INVESTMENT

Diamonds may not be a good investment for the average person, but they certainly aren't a *bad* investment. If a diamond is purchased at the right price, it will most certainly hold its value. Since the diamond crash of 1979, when D flawless diamonds fell in value from seventy-five thousand dollars to under fifteen thousand dollars, the price of diamonds has been increasing constantly.

12. NO DIAMOND IS PERFECT

The definition of a perfect diamond would be a diamond free from inclusions and blemishes when viewed under 10X loupe (flawless), with no trace of color (D-color), and perfectly proportioned. Even though they are rare, there are such diamonds around.

13. IT IS DIFFICULT TO TELL THE DIFFERENCE BETWEEN A DIAMOND AND A CUBIC ZIRCONIA

Any good jeweler can tell the difference immediately. A cubic zirconia has more of a plastic look. There seems to be a light—blue cast throughout the entire stone. One sure way to determine the difference is by weighing the cubic zirconia. A cubic zirconia will weigh 75 percent more!

14. DIAMONDS ARE EXPENSIVE

Some are; some aren't. It depends on their quality. Believe it or not, it's possible to get a one-carat diamond for as low as three hundred dollars if it's junky enough.

15. DIAMONDS ARE A GIRL'S BEST FRIEND

This one would have stumped me, too. I've always believed that all women like diamonds. It wasn't until recently that I learned there are some women out there that very much dislike diamonds and think they are a waste of money. I guess for them maybe a dog is their best friend.

HOW TO BUY A DIAMOND

CHAPTER SEVEN

INSURING & CLEANING YOUR PURCHASE

O NCE you own the ring, you have to take care of it as you would take care of any major investment.

INSURANCE

As soon as you get home with the ring, take steps to get it insured. If you don't already have an insurance company, start shopping for one. Many insurance companies will only insure personal jewelry if you have a homeowner's or renter's policy with them. If you have to shop for an insurance company, use this questionnaire.

1. Name of company: _____

2. Will they insure jewelry? Yes _____ No _____

3. If yes, under what conditions will they insure jewelry?

_____

4. What is the cost of the insurance, per year, per $100 of value?

_____

5. Do they need an appraisal, or will the sales

receipt do? _____

6. Do they need a photograph of the jewelry? _____

7. Does the policy cover loss, theft and damage? _____

8. Does the policy cover replacement value at the time of the loss?

_____

9. Following a loss, does the insurance company pay the insured amount, or replace the lost article with a new one? _____

DOS AND DON'TS

- *Don't* let people touch your diamonds. People seem to have an overwhelming desire to touch a pretty ring. Politely tell them, look but don't touch. Oil from their fingers will quickly dim the brilliance of the stone, and the oil makes it easier for airborne dirt to stick to the diamond.

- *Do* clean the ring *daily*! Diamonds just don't look good when they're dirty (see p. 118, *Cleaning Your Diamond*).

- *Don't* wear the ring in the bath or shower. Soap scum

gets trapped under the prongs and can make the diamond look dull. Also, it's too easy to whack the ring against the tub or shower stall, possibly damaging the ring or loosening the diamond.

- *Don't* be tempted by jewelry store window offers of "Free Jewelry Cleaning." Never leave your jewelry with a jeweler you don't know and trust. Unfortunately, there are jewelers who would use this opportunity to switch your diamond for a fake. Or they might not know what they're doing and damage your jewelry accidentally while cleaning it.

SOME FINAL SUGGESTIONS

1. Don't make an engagement ring a birthday or Christmas gift. First, if on the off chance she were to break up with you and the engagement ring was a birthday or Christmas gift, then she would be able to keep the ring. Second, the giving of an engagement ring should be on a special day all by itself — for example, on the one year anniversary of your first date. The more thought and preparation you put into this, the more it will be appreciated.

2. Once you've purchased the ring, as tempting as it might be to want to show off your purchase to your friends and family, don't. The showing off is for your girlfriend to do once she gets the ring. What you don't want happening is for everyone to say, "Oh, yes, that's pretty; we've seen it before!" One of

117

the most exciting parts about receiving an engagement ring is showing it off and watching your friends and family's reaction to seeing it for the first time. Don't take that away from her. Once you purchase the diamond, don't show it to anyone. That will be her job.

3. If you can't follow rule two and break down and show the ring to someone and it happens to be a lady, don't — I mean don't — let her try it on. Some women are very superstitious about being the first and sometimes the only one to wear the ring. You don't want your wife-to-be to run into this person and have her say, "Oh, yes, I saw it last week and tried it on and told your fiancée that if it looks good on me it will look good on you!" You're a dead man if this happens, and all the money you spent on the ring will go down the drain!

CLEANING YOUR DIAMOND (AND OTHER JEWELS)

You can keep your jewelry sparkling clean at home with a little time and effort, but you should also take your jewelry to your jeweler twice a year for a professional cleaning and to have the stones checked to make sure the setting is tight.

The easiest method of home cleaning is ultrasonic. An ultrasonic cleaner sends sonic waves through a cleaning solution to literally vibrate the dirt off your jewelry. Every morning you can place your jewelry into the cleaner and in ten minutes the jewelry is ready to wear. You can buy an ultrasonic cleaner for under $50 in specialty stores. If you have a hard time finding one, write to me c/o Sourcebooks and I'll have one shipped to you.

Not all ultrasonic cleaners are safe for all gemstones. Read the directions to be sure yours is safe for your jewelry.

Jewelry Cleaning Discovery

Ronald Lockhart from Downingtown, Pennsylvania has invented an ingenious product called the "Powerescent Tablet." Here's how it works: you place the jewelry to be cleaned in a bowl or glass, add hot water, then drop in the Alka Selzer-like tablet. Ten minutes later, ba-boom. Jewelry is clean! Let me tell you. I really love this product! Since it is not an ammonia-based solution, it's safe and easy to use on all jewelry including pearls and emeralds. It's also great for travel. An ultrasonic cleaner can be difficult to take on the road, but these tablets are a piece of cake!

You can also clean your jewelry by hand. Purchase a plastic container with a lid (24 oz.), a bottle of Parson's Sudsy Ammonia, and a medium toothbrush. Fill the container with two parts water, one part ammonia. (Keep the lid on this solution — the fumes are pretty strong!) Each day, place the jewelry in this solution and let it soak for at least ten minutes. Take the jewelry out of the solution and scrub it with the toothbrush, making sure you scrub *underneath* as well as on top. Rinse with warm water, shake off the excess water, then dry with a lint-free cloth.

JEWELRY CARE GUIDE

GEMSTONE	RECOMMENDED	WHAT TO AVOID
Amethyst	Any ultrasonic; bristle brush*	Nothing
Aquamarine	Some ultrasonics**; bristle brush	Some ultrasonics
Citrine	Any ultrasonic; bristle brush	Nothing
Diamond	Any ultrasonic; bristle brush	Sharp blows
Emerald	Warm soapy water; bristle brush	Jewelry cleaner; household chemicals; treated cloth; sharp blows; extreme temperature changes; some ultrasonics
Garnet	Some ultrasonics; bristle brush	Jewelry cleaner; household chemicals; treated cloth; sharp blows; extreme temperature changes; some ultrasonics

Gemstone	Recommended	What to Avoid
Onyx	Any ultrasonic; bristle brush	Sharp blows
Peridot	Some ultrasonics; bristle brush	Jewelry cleaner; household chemicals treated cloth; sharp blows; extreme temperature changes; some ultrasonics
Ruby	Any ultrasonic; bristle brush	Nothing
Sapphire	Any ultrasonic; bristle brush	Nothing
Tanzanite	Some ultrasonics; bristle brush	Jewelry cleaner; household chemicals; treated cloth; sharp blows; extreme temperature changes; some ultrasonics
Topaz	Some ultrasonics; bristle brush	Jewelry cleaner; household chemicals; treated cloth; sharp blows; extreme temperature changes; some ultrasonics
Tourmaline	Some ultrasonics; bristle brush	Some ultrasonics
Tsavorite	Some ultrasonics; bristle brush	Jewelry cleaner; household chemicals; treated cloth; sharp blows; extreme temperature changes; some ultrasonics

GEMSTONE	RECOMMENDED	WHAT TO AVOID
Zircon	Some ultrasonics; bristle brush	Sharp blows; some ultrasonics
24K Gold	Any ultrasonic	Treated cloth; sharp blows; scratching

* I recommend a medium toothbrush.

** Some ultrasonic cleaners may damage certain stones. Check the directions that come with your cleaner.

CHAPTER EIGHT

"WILL YOU MARRY ME?"

THOSE four little words form what may well be the most important question you'll ever ask. The rest of your life flows from that question. It joins two families and begins a new family, and determines everything from what you'll eat for dinner, to where you'll spend your holidays, to what your children will be like.

In other words, this question is a BIG DEAL! Too big to treat casually. You don't want to just pull out the ring box while you're watching TV and say, "Oh, yeah, I thought you might like to, uh, y'know... would you?"

Make it a moment you'll both remember forever!

She will remember it, every tiny detail of it — the weather, what she was wearing, what you were wearing, the time, the place, *everything*. She'll remember who she told first, and what they said, and how her parents reacted, and how your parents reacted — *everything*. So take the time and make the effort to plan it, and make the details come out right. Why spend a lot of time and money getting the perfect diamond only to have the Big Moment turn out to be a flop? The diamond is just one part of the Perfect Proposal. It takes thought, planning, loving attention to detail, and occasionally teamwork to create the kind of fireworks that will leave a lasting glow on your lives together.

PLANNING THE PERFECT PROPOSAL: A WORKSHEET

Attire   Will you wear a tux? Maybe a gorilla suit to say that you're not monkeying around? Make a statement with your wardrobe.

Budget   Do you rent a plane or a limo? Take her to the most romantic restaurant? Feed her champagne and caviar? Determine what you can afford to spend on a once-in-a-lifetime occasion.

Location   Very important! The observation deck of the tallest building in town? A hilltop under the stars? On the deck of a sailboat? On a moonlit beach? Don't forget, it can be a "combo": first a restaurant, then the beach, for example.

Day & Time   Pick a day that's special to you, such as the anniversary of your first date. Or evening, when a full moon rises over the lake.

Food   Taking her to the first restaurant you went to together can be fun. Cooking her a meal is a sure winner!

Flowers   Absolutely! Whether it's great bouquets of flowers or a single red rose, flowers are a must for romantic moments.

Candy   Find out what her favorite is, and present it as a treasure, wrapped in gold paper and tied with a bow, even if it's a Snickers bar.

Accessories Take along a cellular phone so she can call her mother or her sister. She'll be bursting to tell everyone! If you can, set up a video camera to record the moment.

Scrapbook Write down all the details of the moment — details that you (and your children) will savor in years to come. Include newspaper headlines from the day you got engaged.

Engagement Facts

- Approximately 2,400,000 couples wed in the U.S. each year.
- One third of all couples become engaged during the last quarter of the year, October through December.
- The average age of a man getting engaged is 26.5 years; the woman's average engagement age is 24.4.
- The average price of a diamond engagement ring is $1,597. If the engagement ring is purchased as part of a bridal set, the average price is $880.

FIVE PROPOSAL STYLES

Over the years I've come across five basic styles of proposals. Which best describes your situation?

The Total Surprise

She doesn't know it's coming — not a clue, not a hint. You've never even discussed it. This is gutsy! It reminds me of the school dances of my youth, where all the girls were on one side of the gym and all the boys stood on the other. You'd finally get up the nerve to make that long walk across the floor to ask a girl to dance. If she said "No," and they often did, the walk back across the floor was very, very long.

I figure fewer than 10% of all proposals are in this category. It's like doing a high-wire act without a net. Most guys drop hints first, or get hints from her which indicate which way the wind is blowing.

But there are the big risk-takers, the guys who live on the edge, who just go out and buy the ring and make the dinner reservations and GO FOR IT! Hurrah for them, but — *I have to tell you I don't recommend popping the question "cold."*

Great Proposals, #1

"Beach Party"

On a warm September evening, Peter takes Susan to dinner at their favorite restaurant, the dining room of an elegant inn on the coast of Maine. The maitre d' tells them their table will be ready in a half-hour, and suggests a stroll on the beach while they wait. As they amble down the short path from the inn to the beach in the soft last light of the day, they hear violins playing "their song." On the beach they find a string quartet in tuxedos playing to a table, candlelit and elegantly set for two, with a vase of red roses in the center and a bottle of champagne chilling in a silver ice bucket. When they reach the table, Susan gasps as she reads the place cards: "Susan" and "Peter." They sit, Susan's amazement growing by the minute. Peter pours champagne and offers a toast to their love, then pulls a particular red rose from the vase and presents it to her. She inhales the fragrance of the rose, then, as she discovers the beautiful diamond ring tied to the stem of the rose with a white silk ribbon, she hears the magic words: "Will you marry me?"

She Knows

You've talked about getting married, you know you both want to get married and spend your lives together, you've talked about having kids, you've pledged your undying love. The only thing she *doesn't* know is when it's coming.

Men, the time between when she knows you'll give her a ring and the moment when you actually give it to her can be one of the greatest times of your life. Have some fun! Keep her guessing, plan the moment well, and when she least expects it, spring your wonderful surprise.

Great Proposals, #2

"Breakast at Tiffany's"

One Saturday morning, Sam picks up his girlfriend Marie. They have planned to run errands, but instead Sam takes her to a jewelry store where the sales manager escorts them to a private room. There, Marie finds a table set with candles, flowers and champagne — plus a selection of six diamond engagement rings, all in her size, arranged on a fine china plate. Sam drops to one knee, and proposes. Marie happily accepts, and Sam pulls out a chair for her, pours a glass of champagne, and tells her to choose her engagement ring — any one of the beautiful sparklers on the plate before her.

Let's Elope!

"Will you marry me? Right now? Tonight?"

Wow! This one makes no sense to me unless:

- The Early Pregnancy Test came up positive

- America's Most Wanted is profiling you tonight

- It's her fifth marriage, your seventh

- You don't want to give her a chance to change her mind

- Desert Storm II has broken out and you've been called up

- You love her so much you just can't wait

It's Now or Never

Way to go — you've waited so long she's resorting to threats: "We're getting married or I'll find someone who'll appreciate me!" Fish or cut bait, guy. If you love her, get off the fence and show her you can't live without her. If it's come to the threatening stage, you have to be extra, extra romantic to make up for her long wait. Use my proposal planning guide on page 124 and make it a great one!

❧ Great Proposals, #3 ❧

Nicole raced home from work early to get ready for a romantic evening on the town with her boyfriend, Devin. It was her birthday! He had told her to "dress up," because he was taking her to a fancy restaurant . At the appointed hour, the doorbell rang, and in stepped Devin in a snazzy tux, bearing roses and an armload of gifts. He produced a bottle of champagne and suggested they sit on the couch, drink a toast to her birthday, and she could open her birthday gifts.

The first gift was a new dress that Devin had picked out for her. She loved it! She opened the next present — a sexy negligée. Then came a new best-selling novel (she's a voracious reader). Finally, Devin handed her a small, elegantly-wrapped box. Nicole's eyebrows raised a millimeter or two — it was obviously a jewelry box, and she loves jewelry. She carefully removed the wrapping to discover the familiar blue box that is Tiffany's hallmark, and her heart beat just a tiny bit faster. Opening the box, she saw winking up at her a sterling silver key ring with a sterling heart pendant, and on the heart was engraved — her birthdate. How romantic! But there was a much bigger surprise in store. When she took the key ring from its little box she turned it over and looked at the other side of the heart. Engraved on that side were the words, "Marry me!"

Ringless

You and your True Love are in each other's arms, caught up in a rising tide of passion. The dialogue goes like this:

"Honey, I love you!"
"I love you, too, sweetheart."
(Kiss kiss smooch kiss)
"I can't live without you!"
"Oh, baby, you're the only one I'll ever love!"
(Smooch kiss smooch kiss)
"Will you marry me?"
"Yes!, Oh, yes yes yes!"

But does Romeo have a ring in his pocket? Nooooooo. So where do we go from here?

Don't think this lets you out of getting her a ring! Get that thought out of your head right now!

A lot of Ringless Proposals lead to a couple shopping together for the ring. Or, you could revert to the "She Knows" proposal and keep her guessing. *Either way, the Ringless Proposal shouldn't be ringless for long.*

Great Proposals, #4

"The Twelve Days of Love"

This is a romantic variation on the Twelve Days of Christmas, in reverse. Twelve days before he planned to propose to Ellen, Tim began sending her gifts. Each day, a limo would arrive, and a uniformed butler would step out bearing an anonymous gift. First, twelve red roses. Then came eleven love poems, ten pieces of Godiva chocolate, nine porcelain boxes, eight champagne flutes, seven cuddly teddy bears, six silk scarves, five silver charms, four scented soaps, three bottles of perfume, two pearl earrings — and finally, on the twelfth day, Tim arrived in person, dressed as the butler, bearing one bottle of champagne, one Very Important Question, and one diamond ring.

Great Proposals, #5

"On the Radio"

Dave called the evening DJ at the radio station he and Tina always listened to and enlisted his collaboration. Friday evening, as Dave and Tina were in the car, heading for dinner at their favorite restaurant, the DJ began playing the pre-recorded interview he'd done with Dave. On the tape, Dave is telling the DJ about his wonderful girlfriend, and the story of how they met, and everything about her. Tina gradually realizes that this story sounds familiar. Then she realizes it's Dave's voice she's hearing on the radio! Dave continues driving, grinning from ear to ear as Tina listens in astonishment. Finally, over the radio, Dave's voice says, "Tina, open the glove compartment." She does, and finds a ring box. "Open it," Dave's voice commands. Inside is a beautiful diamond ring. Finally, Dave's voice comes over the radio asking, "Tina, will you marry me?"

HOW TO BUY A DIAMOND

CHAPTER NINE

BUYING YOUR 2ND, 3RD, OR 4TH DIAMOND

THERE'S a very good chance that the diamond engagement ring won't be the last diamond you buy! Perhaps you're already looking for your second diamond. In my experience, there are five main reasons people shop for another diamond: Remarriage, Replacement, Upgrade, Trade-in and Special Occasion.

NEW MARRIAGE

Marriages end, sad to say, by death or divorce, but love can bloom again! New love, at any age, brings springtime back into your heart and pretty soon you find yourself gazing into jewelry store windows. Now I'm going to give you one piece of advice which will spare you a lot of grief.

Love is beautiful the second time around — but the ring isn't! Never recycle or even duplicate the ring from your previous marriage.

God forbid you should ever recycle a ring that you gave to a former fiancée or an ex-wife. Never!

Your new love wants to feel special, wants to know that there's never been a love such as her. You'll shatter that feeling if you give her a ring from a previous relationship.

Of course, the exception is a family heirloom, perhaps your mother's or grandmother's ring — but not if it was also worn by your former wife. If you do give your beloved an heirloom ring, she's entitled to a new setting if she wants one. It's only the diamond that's forever. If your family has a problem with a setting change, it might be best to leave the heirloom in safe deposit and purchase a new ring.

Diamond Factoid

The country which produces the most diamonds, both by weight and by number: Australia! (40 million +).

REPLACEMENT DIAMOND

If her first diamond is lost, stolen or damaged you'll be shopping for a replacement. Don't assume she'll want an exact replica! Some women love the original so much they will want exactly the same thing if the original is gone, but other women will be ready for a change. Tastes do change over time, after all, so talk this over. Be diplomatic, and give her the option of change. Say to her, "Honey, I know your old ring meant a lot to you, and it

136

meant a lot to me, and I'd do anything to bring it back, but it's gone. And since we're doing (a little)(a lot)(tons!) better than we were then, I want this ring to be all you want it to be. So I'll be happy to get you a duplicate of the old ring, or a new one that's bigger, better, or just different. The choice is yours — I just want you to be happy." You'll be a hero!

If the old diamond was damaged so that the clarity grade has dropped by two grades or more, the insurance company should cover the cost of replacement. If your damaged diamond was not insured, maybe you can still use it as a trade-in.

DIAMOND UPGRADES

This can be an upgrade in size, quality or both. Many women are happy with their original ring but would still like to have a new, bigger one. An anniversary is an ideal time to make this upgrade. This is another time to be practical and talk things over together. Does she want to trade in the original, or want to keep the original and get a new one? Many women treasure their original engagement ring, and even if they get a bigger diamond later, they want to keep the original and wear it as a pendant or save it for a child's future engagement. Or, some women will take a more practical approach and use the trade-in value of the original to get an even larger new diamond.

Fred's advice: Never trade in her existing engagement ring without her knowledge!

137

TRADE-INS

Diamonds for trade-in can come from a lot of places. Your wife's old engagement ring, a ring from a failed engagement, former marriage or a family heirloom. The keys to getting the most for your trade-in are as follows:

1. Get an independent appraisal of the trade-in diamond and ask the appraiser for the Rapaport value of the stone. "Rapaport" is a price sheet all appraisers use to determine a diamond's wholesale value. The Rapaport value = wholesale price; retail is 2X Rapaport. You should always be able to buy a diamond at its Rapaport price, and receive credit on a trade-in at Rapaport.

2. After you get the appraisal, you can visit your jeweler knowing what you should get for the trade-in. Don't be lazy and let the jeweler appraise the diamond. A lot of jewelers might undervalue your trade-in.

3. Jewelers hate trade-ins, so always negotiate your new purchase *before* indicating you have a trade-in. If you tell the jeweler up front you have a trade, he'll just jack up the retail price.

•Determine what type and grade of diamond you want

•Negotiate the price, using the guidelines in this book

- Show your trade-in, telling the jeweler you've already gotten an independent appraisal

- Make sure the trade-in amount equals the appraised value

- Subtract the trade-in value from the price you negotiated for the new diamond, and that's your bottom line.

Example:

You're buying a 1.49ct SI1, Class 2, no fluorescence.
Price: $7,152
Your trade-in is a .50ct VS1-J
Appraised value: $1,350
You pay: $5,802

SPECIAL OCCASIONS & GIFTS

As time goes by, you'll want to add to her diamond collection with gifts for a birthday, Christmas or Chanukah, an anniversary or some other special day. This might mean diamond stud earrings, a diamond tennis bracelet, a pendant, or an anniversary ring. The #1 question I'm asked about these purchases is, "Do I get the same quality as the engagement diamond?" Well, my friend, how important is the purchase to you? Most people see the engagement ring as something they'll treasure for a lifetime. Is that how you view this new purchase? If so, don't waste your money on second-class merchandise. If not, get a cubic zirconia or costume jewelry. The decision is yours.

Trunk Shows

Many jewelers offer what are known as "remount trunk shows." These are basically marketing events at which they offer hundreds of settings, and where jewelers try to entice you to replace or trade in your old diamond. The problem with a trunk show is that all the diamonds have been mounted in settings, so it's impossible to check their weight, clarity and color. And don't ever trade in your old diamond at these shows — they'll probably undervalue it.

Fred's Advice: Never buy a diamond in a prefabricated setting for more than $2,000 unless the jeweler will let you view the diamonds loose.

CHAPTER TEN

How to
Sell a Diamond

I KNOW this book is called "How to Buy a Diamond," but let's face it: not all diamonds are forever. There may come a time in your life when you want to sell a diamond or two, for one reason or another. It may be an engagement ring from a previous marriage, or a pair of diamond studs from an ex-boyfriend. It may be a family heirloom, or just a diamond you don't wear anymore. Rather than let it gather dust in your safe deposit box, you'd like to convert it to cold cash. Here's what you need to do. And remember: Patience is a virtue! If you rush into a sale without doing your homework, you'll get burned. Follow these steps:

Step 1: Appraisal

Have the diamond appraised. You need to know what you have, and a qualified appraiser can tell you. Find one by calling the Appraisers Association of America, 386 Park Avenue South, Suite 2000, New York City, NY 10016, at (212) 889-5404. Tell them where you live, and ask for a list of appraisers in your area. They won't tell you over the phone, but they'll send you a few recommendations — it'll take about a week. If you'd like their complete membership directory, they'll mail it to you for $14.95. If you can't wait, look in the Yellow Pages under Appraisers. Check the appraiser's affiliations. The top three groups are:

Appraisers Association of America

American Society of Appraisers

International Society of Appraisers

Membership in any of these is a good indication the appraiser is okay.

Step 2: Rapaport Value

Ask the appraiser for the Rapaport value. Rapaport is a wholesale price sheet published in New York that tells jewelry stores all over the country the prices they should pay for diamonds. The Rapaport prices are wholesale, just like the prices in this book. *The price the appraiser gives you will be the highest price you can get for your diamond.* For example, if your diamond is a 1-carat, round, VS1-G, Class 2 cut with no fluorescence, the Rapaport value would be $6,200. That's the most you'll get for it. That same diamond would sell for more in a jewelry store, but you're not a jewelry store! Anyone who buys a diamond from an individual, who gives no guarantees or warranties, is simply looking for a good deal.

Step 3: Buyers

Find a buyer. There are a number of possibilities here, but I'm going to firmly guide you away from most of them. In my mind, the two best choices are: 1) Family or friend, and 2) a jeweler.

A. Family or friend:

This is my top recommendation hands down. I've seen people try every which way to sell a diamond or piece of jewelry, then finally discover that a family member or friend would love to buy it. Before you go to strangers, look close to home for a buyer. You'll always make your best deal with someone who knows you, loves your jewelry and wants to own it, while a liquidator just wants to resell it for a quick buck.

B. Jewelry store:

Yes, but be careful! Never let the jewelry out of your sight — you don't want someone pulling a "switcheroo" on you. Before the jeweler starts a spiel about how poor your diamond is, show him the appraisal. At that point, the jeweler will probably make you an offer that is below "dump value." Dump value is a trade expression — it means 60-80% of the diamond's Rapaport value, and it's the lowest price a diamond should ever sell for. If the jeweler offers you *below* 60%, don't take it. He's going for a fast buck, because he knows he can resell the stone overnight to a dealer at regular dump value. But if the jeweler offers you 60-80% of the Rapaport value, he's actually being fair.

Remember, to make any money from the deal he'll have to find a new buyer for the diamond, and who knows what expenses he'll incur to do that.

Let's take our 1-carat VS1-G, Class 2 cut diamond from Step 2, which has a Rapaport (wholesale) value of $6,200. Dump value would be 60-80% of that, or between $3,720 and $4,960. Try to negotiate the best price, of course, but don't feel insulted if the jeweler's offer is 5% below the low dump price. He's just trying to make a little money for handling the deal. But if he offers you only 40% or even 50% of wholesale, tell him NO DEAL!

Now let's talk about some options that I do NOT recommend.

C. Newspapers:

The premise is simple: you take out an ad, a buyer calls you and gives you money for your diamond. But it's never that simple. I have seen the classified ads work, but not often. In fact, I did a little survey on my own and found only an 11% success rate. You can do better than that in Las Vegas! Furthermore, placing an ad exposes you to all sorts of people including crooks who want to steal your jewelry. You'll make appointment after appointment with "buyers" who don't show up. Even if you attract a legitimate buyer, he'll drag you back to the appraiser and then make a ridiculous offer. I would avoid the classifieds. It's not worth putting yourself in danger.

144

❦ Diamond Mystique at Work ❧

The diamond weighed forty carats. It was discovered in Lesotho, South Africa, and had been cut into a Marquise shape and mounted as a spectacular ring. The clarity grade was high — VVS — but the color was only M or N, and at wholesale the diamond would fetch perhaps $260,000. But when the ring sold at auction in April 1996, the winning bid was $2.58 million — ten times the wholesale value! Why? Because this was the ring Aristotle Onassis gave to the widow of President John F. Kennedy as an engagement ring, and bidding at the Sotheby's auction of the Jacqueline Kennedy Onassis estate was a feeding frenzy by the well-heeled who wanted to touch and own a piece of Camelot. For the high bidder, Anthony J. F. O'Reilly, the ring had a special appeal. His wife Chryss was a Goulandris, a member of a powerful Greek family that had been an archrival of the Onassis family in the shipping business.

D. On consignment:

A jeweler might say, "Hey, why not leave your diamond with me and I'll sell it on consignment and make big money for you." DON'T DO IT!! NEVER leave your jewelry with anyone unless you're paid up front. He can promise you the moon, switch your good diamond for a piece of junk or a cubic zirconia, then call you in a couple of weeks to tell you to pick up your jewelry because he couldn't sell it!

E. Pawn shops:

They should be called "Prawn Shops," because they'll dip you in cocktail sauce and eat you alive. On average, pawnbrokers will offer you only 10% of wholesale. STAY AWAY!!

You may have heard of *Diamond Dealer Clubs*, but these are only for the trade, and unless you're in the trade you won't get within ten feet of these places.

Another option, for high-end jewelry only, is an *auction house*. The top two in the U.S. are:

> Christie's
> 502 Park Avenue at 59th Street
> New York City, NY 10022
> (212) 546-1000
>
> Sotheby's
> 1334 York Avenue
> New York City, NY 10021
> (212) 606-7000

ANTIQUE OR "ESTATE" JEWELRY

Many people love to shop for antique jewelry, in hopes of finding a beautiful and unique piece of jewelry, softly glowing with

146

the patina of time and enhanced by the mystique of history. Fine, but remember that buying previously-owned jewelry is a lot like buying a used car. Be smart enough to get a trained mechanic to look under the hood — that is, get an independent appraisal, and follow the guidelines in this book just as if you were buying a new piece of jewelry.

There are two things to be careful of. One, a lot of antique diamonds are Old Mine or Old European cuts. These styles, popular in the late 1800s and early 1900s, are cut very high and deep and allow a lot of light to leak out the bottom. They really are nothing better than a Class 3 or Class 4 cut diamond. If you're buying an antique diamond with one of these cuts, expect a 35-40% discount off the prices listed in this book.

The second caution is, watch out for fairy tales! Dealers know that a diamond with a fascinating history is going to sell faster and for a higher price than one without a history. Don't be mesmerized by tales of Russian princesses or Arab sultans. Listen politely and smile, but then say, "That's great, but it's still a VS1-G, Class 3 cut!"

CHAPTER ELEVEN

ANNIVERSARIES
AND OCCASIONS

I f there's any man out there who believes that his jewelry-
buying days are over after he purchases the bridal set — let
me dispel that notion here and now! The fire in that first diamond always ignites a burning desire for more. "My engagement
ring is lonely," she'll say. "It needs diamond earrings to keep it
company." Or a tennis bracelet, or a pendant — the list goes on.

Anniversaries are perfect times for gifts of jewelry, gifts that say
"you'd marry her all over again," to quote from the advertise-
ment. *Never* make the mistake of getting your spouse a *practical*
anniversary gift, like a new toaster or a vacuum cleaner.
Anniversaries are occasions to celebrate and renew your love
for each other, and only a personal gift such as jewelry is right
for the moment.

Here's a traditional anniversary gift list.

Anniversary	Gift
1	Clocks
2	China
3	Crystal, glass
4	Electrical appliances (Yuck!)
5	Silverware
6	Wood
7	Pen & pencil set
8	Linen, lace
9	Leather
10	Diamond jewelry
11	Fashion jewelry
12	Pearls or colored stones
13	Textiles, furs
14	Gold jewelry
15	Watches
16	Silver hollowware
17	Furniture
18	Porcelain
19	Bronze
20	Platinum
25	Sterling Silver Jubilee
30	Diamond
35	Jade
40	Ruby
45	Sapphire
50	Golden Jubilee
55	Emerald
60	Diamond Jubilee

Here's a Gem Anniversary List, developed by several trade associations.

ANNIVERSARY	GIFT
1	Gold jewelry
2	Garnet (all colors)
3	Pearls
4	Blue Topaz
5	Sapphire (all colors)
6	Amethyst
7	Onyx
8	Tourmaline
9	Lapis
10	Diamond jewelry
11	Turquoise
12	Jade
13	Citrine
14	Opal
15	Ruby
16	Peridot
17	Watches
18	Cat's Eye
19	Aquamarine
20	Emerald
21	Iolite
22	Spinel (all colors)
23	Imperial Topaz
24	Tanzanite
25	Sterling Silver Jubilee
30	Pearl Jubilee
35	Emerald
40	Ruby
45	Sapphire
50	Golden Jubilee
55	Alexandrite
60	Diamond Jubilee

NATURAL BIRTHSTONES

January	Garnet	A red lustrous stone which occurs mainly as crystals.
February	Amethyst	A clear purple or bluish violet variety of quartz crystal.
March	Aquamarine	A transparent beryl that may be blue, blue-green or green in color.
April	Diamond	Need we say more?
May	Emerald	A rich green variety of beryl, highly prized.
June	Pearl	Dense, lustrous layers of nacre formed around a foreign object within the shell of oysters and some other mollusks.
July	Ruby	A rare red corundum, sometimes worth $30,000 per carat.
August	Peridot	A deep yellowish-green olivine stone.
September	Sapphire	A rich blue transparent corundum gemstone.
October	Opal	A hydrated silica gemstone noted for its iridescent play of colors.
November	Topaz	A silicate of aluminum, usually a transparent yellow to brownish-yellow.
December	Turquoise	A sky-blue copper aluminum phosphate, highly prized.

And In Conclusion

ONGRATULATIONS! You have finished *How to Buy a Diamond*. You've learned about the Four C's, how to grade diamonds, how to select a jeweler and how to get the best diamond for your dollar. You have your questionnaire sheets to guide you. Now, I want you to ask yourself two more questions:

Do I really want to marry her?

Does she really want to marry me?

If you don't answer these questions immediately and emphatically "YES!!" then maybe you should think this over before you make a serious investment in a ring that says "Forever." Marriage is a magnificent institution for two people in love who have no doubts about wholehearted commitment to one another. Please be sure you're in that category before visiting the jeweler.

I hope you've had as much fun reading this book as I have had writing it. I know that buying a diamond can be one of the most expensive and nerve-wracking purchases you'll ever make, but it can also be one of the most exciting and rewarding — if you apply the lessons you've learned in this book. Follow my advice, and you should be able to get the right diamond at the right-price. And isn't that what it's all about?

HAPPY DIAMOND SHOPPING!

Appendix

THE ALPHABET RULES: L-M-N-O-P

Recently I appeared on a PBS special about diamonds, and the producer asked me if I could come up with 4 or 5 easy-to-remember rules for diamond shopping. So I came up with the Alphabet Rules, a quick and simple consumer protection guide that will help even a novice avoid getting ripped off.

L = Loose	Always look at loose, not mounted, diamonds. The setting may hide flaws.
M = Magnify	Always look at your diamond through a jeweler's loupe or a microscope, which will reveal imperfections invisible to the naked eye.
N = Negotiate	Most retailers dramatically increase prices. Never pay the sticker price unless you've shopped around and you know they're already giving you a wholesale price.
O = Opinion	Always insist that the final sale be contingent upon the opinion of an independent appraiser. If the appraiser agrees you've done well, the sale will be final.
P = Plot	Always have the diamond's flaws plotted on a drawing of the stone. That way you'll be able to identify your diamond by the location of its blemishes and inclusions.

CARAT SIZE CHARTS

CARAT WEIGHT	SHAPES		
.50			
.75			
1.00			
1.25			
1.50			
2.00			
2.50			
3.00			
4.00			
5.00			

155

Carat Weight	Round	Carat Weight	Round
1/150	∘	1.00	◯
1/100	∘		
1/70	∘	1.25	◯
1/50	∘	1.50	◯
1/40	○	1.75	◯
1/33	○		
1/25	○	3.00	◯
.03	◉		
.05	○	4.00	◯
.07	○		
.10	○	5.00	◯
.15	○		
.20	○		
.25	○	6.00	◯
.33	○		
.40	○	7.00	◯
.50	○		
.65	○		
.75	○		
.85	○		

Glossary of Terms

SPEAKING THE JEWELER'S LANGUAGE

Blemish   A flaw on the exterior of a diamond, such as a scratch, abrasion, nick or chip.

Blue-white   Refers to a diamond that glows (flouresces) blue under ultraviolet light.

Brilliance   White light reflected back from a diamond.

Brilliant   A round diamond with 58 facets.

Carat   A unit of weight, equal to 200 milligrams. In ancient times one carat was equal to one carob bean or four grains of rice.

Carbon   The raw material of which diamonds are made. Occasionally a diamond will contain tiny pockets of carbon which can be seen as black spots within the stone.

Cloud   A cluster of small inclusions, or internal flaws, within a diamond.

Crown   The top of a diamond. Everything above the girdle.

Culet   The bottom facet of a diamond, usually very small.

Dispersion	Colored light reflected from within a diamond; also called "fire."
Eye-clean	Refers to a diamond that has no inclusions or blemishes visible to the naked eye.
Facet	A polished surface on a diamond. A round, full-cut diamond usually has 58 facets.
Fluorescence	A diamond's reaction to ultraviolet (UV) light, causing the stone to glow in various colors.
Full-cut	A diamond with 58 or more facets.
Gemologist	A person who has been trained and certified in diamonds and colored stones.
GIA	Gemological Institute of America, an independent, non-profit organization which sets and upholds standards for grading diamonds and other precious stones.
Girdle	The narrow, unpolished band around the widest part of the diamond; the girdle separates the crown and the pavilion of the stone.
Head	The prongs which hold a diamond in its setting.
Inclusion	A flaw within a diamond, such as carbon spots or fractures.

Karat	The measure of the purity of gold; 24-karat being pure gold. Jewelry is usually made from 18K and 14K gold, which contain other metals for strength.
Laser-drilled	A diamond that has been treated with a laser to remove carbon spots.
Loupe	A small magnifying glass used to view gemstones
Off-make	A poorly proportioned diamond.
Pavé	A method of setting diamonds very closely together, giving the illusion of one or more larger diamonds.
Pavilion	The bottom of a diamond; everything below the diamond's girdle.
Point	One-hundredth of a carat. A diamond weighing one-and-a-half carats weighs 150 points.
Semi-mount	A setting which is complete except for the main stone, which will be selected separately.
Single-cut	A diamond with only 16 or 17 facets.
Sparkle	The liveliness of the light reflecting from a diamond; the sum of the brilliance and the fire (dispersion).
Tiffany	A simple, elegant 2-3mm ring setting with a head that holds a single diamond.

101 Ways to Be Romantic

As a bonus for the romantic readers of *How To Buy A Diamond*, here are one-hundred-and-one of Gregory J.P. Godek's favorite romantic ideas, selected from his bestseller *1001 Ways To Be Romantic*. Enjoy!

ROMANCE 101

1   Call your lover every hour on the hour . . . all day long! . . . just to say "I love you."

2   Don't bother with a dozen roses . . . one is plenty! But make sure you attach a personal and heartfelt note. Maybe the lyrics to her favorite love song.

3   Save the little slips of paper from Hershey's Kisses. Give them to your partner along with a note that says: "These are Love Coupons — each one is redeemable for one kiss."

4   Without a doubt the most romantic show on TV: *Mad About You.*

ROMANCE IS ABOUT THE LITTLE THINGS.
Be Creative!

5   Make your own greeting cards. You don't have to be artistic—just heartfelt!

6   Hiding places for notes and small gifts: Under the pillow, in the glove compartment, in her briefcase, in his sock drawer, in a pizza box, in the refrigerator.

BECOME AN ARTIST OF YOUR RELATIONSHIP

7   Create a "Romantic Idea Jar": Write 100 romantic ideas on separate slips of paper. Fill a jar with them. Once a week you take turns picking one idea at random.

BE PREPARED!

8   Be prepared for spontaneous romantic escapes! Have "His" and "Hers" overnight bags packed at all times. Keep under the bed or in the car trunk.

9   Be prepared for shopping! Know all of your partner's sizes, favorite colors, favorite styles and favorite authors.

10   Be prepared—for anything! Always have on hand: candles, "Love" stamps, good wine, bubblebath and greeting cards.

Great relationships require equal parts of passion, commitment and intimacy.

THE WEIRD AND WACKY

11   Write "I LOVE YOU" on the bathroom mirror with a piece of soap.

12   Eat dinner by candlelight. Heck—eat breakfast by candlelight.

13   Love is timeless—and to prove it, cover-up all the clocks in your house for the entire weekend.

14   Learn to say "I love you" in Japanese ("Ai shite imasu"); in Russian ("Ya lyublyu tyebya"); in Eskimo ("Nagligivaget").

Romance resides in the everyday.

A TOUCH OF CLASS

15   Have her portrait painted from a photograph.

16   Hire a pianist to play during dinner at home!

Love is not a mystery to be solved . . .
it is an experience to be savored.

17   Cook a gourmet dinner for two.

18   Propose a toast to her while at a dinner party with friends.

19   Hire a limousine for an elegant evening out.

ROMANTIC STRATEGIES

20   Overdo something! Does he like m&m's? Buy him 50 pounds of them! Does she like teddy bears? Get her a dozen!

21   Listen! With your ears, mind and heart. Listen for the meaning behind his actions. Listen for the message behind her words.

TIME IS YOUR MOST PRECIOUS COMMODITY
You give yourself when you give your time.

22   Don't wait for holidays to celebrate . . . Celebrate because it's Tuesday! Celebrate the new moon. Celebrate something every week!

ROMANTIC CLASSICS

23   A gold chain and locket—with your picture inside.

24   Dinner at a fine French restaurant.

25   The film classic *Casablanca*.

26   An evening of dancing and dining.

27   A diamond anniversary ring.

Commitment requires daily renewal.

OF NOTE

28   Tape a note to your partner's wristwatch: "Time for love!"

29   Tape a note to the TV: "Turn me on instead!"

Lovers listen with their hearts.

30   Buy a case of wine: Attach a note to each bottle: 1) For our next anniversary, 2) For your birthday, 3) For my birthday, 4) To make up after a fight, 5) . . . [You take it from here!]

31   Write 101 little love notes . . . number them . . . and hide them all over the house.

UNEXPECTED SURPRISES

32   Run out and buy $25 worth of greeting cards. Get a mixture of funny, serious, sexy and romantic cards.

33   Write a love letter. Cut the paper into puzzle-shaped pieces. Mail the pieces to your lover . . . one piece per day!

34   Arrive home from work with a bottle of wine . . . and a big smile!

35   Go for it IN A BIG WAY. Pull out all the stops. Don't tip-toe into being more romantic . . . be outrageously romantic!

The surprise gift is most appreciated.
The unexpected gesture is most treasured.

I Love You

36   Upside down stamps on envelopes mean "I love you."

37   Learn how to say "I love you" using sign language. The book The Joy of Signing, by Lottie Riekoff, will help!

Romance is the expression of love.
It's the "action step"—without which
love is merely an empty concept.

38   For your Romance Library: books with "Love" in their titles:

Love is Letting Go of Fear, by Gerald Jampolsky
Love, by Leo Buscaglia

The Art of Loving, by Erich Fromm

Notes on Love and Courage, by Hugh Prather

LOVESONGS

39 *She Describes Infinity*, a romantic CD by Scott Cossu.

40 *Down To The Moon*, the CD by Andreas Vollenweider.

41 Two wonderful albums available only from the artist:

Illusions and Dreams: On cassette for $12.50
Heart To Heart: Cassette is $12.50; CD is $16.50
Magical acoustic music with original, loving lyrics!
Write to Brit Lay, Box 127, Barnstable, MA 02630.

42 *A Winter's Solstice*, the CD by Windham Hill artists.

Romance is expressing your feelings in your way.

DOS AND DON'TS

43 Guys . . . don't buy women practical gifts! No toasters, blenders or vacuum cleaners!

44 Do plan ahead. Planning doesn't destroy spontaneity, it creates opportunity.

45 Don't give cash as a gift! (Unless it's really a

lot of money!)

46   Don't treat your lover as a stereotype. He's an individual, not a statistic. And she's a unique person, not "just like all women."

The anticipation is often just as much fun as the event or gift itself.

FUN AND GAMES

47   Giftwrap a wishbone in a jewelry box. Send it to your lover with a note that says, "I wish you were here."

Romance is a bridge between the sexes.

48   Kidnap him! Blindfold him; drive him around town until he's thoroughly lost; then reveal your destination: his favorite restaurant, the ballpark, or maybe a romantic inn.

49   Have your handwriting analyzed. Have your astrological charts read. Have your Tarot cards read.

50   Every time you stop at a red light, kiss!

FOR MEN ONLY

51   A shopping trip for men. Buy one item from

each store. Giftwrap each item separately:

Crabtree & Evelyn	A local liquor store
Victoria's Secret	A flower shop
Hallmark Card Shop	A jewelry store

52   Do a household chore that's usually one of "her" jobs.

53   You take the kids out for the afternoon . . . giving her an afternoon of peace and quiet.

54   Shave on Saturday night!

Romance is "Adult Play."

For Women Only

55   Send him a love letter sealed with a kiss. (Use your reddest lipstick.)

Relationships aren't 50/50—they're 100/100.

56   Don't position yourself against his passions. Don't force him to choose between you and his golf/football/cars/fishing. There's time for all of you!

57   Send flowers to him at work.

58   Read Men Are From Mars, Women Are From Venus by John Gray. Cut out your favorite passages and tape them to the refrigerator.

1-800-ROM-ANCE

59   A 50-page catalog of romantic gifts!
      "Marketplace" is full of specially chosen items
      for romantics. Call 800-642-7462.

60   Call 800-322-0344 for the fascinating
      Smithsonian gift catalog. Call 800-435-8863
      for the musical Anyone Can Whistle catalog

61   Go on a romantic cruise! You can reach
      Princess Cruises at 800-LOVEBOAT. Carnival
      Cruises at 800-327-7276. Cunard Line at 800-
      221-4770. Windjammer Cruises at 800-327-
      2601.

62   If he's a science fiction fan, get him TheScience
      Fiction Video Catalog: 800-959-0061. If she's a
      pet lover, get her the Mail Order Pet Shop
      Catalog: 800-326-6677.

The essence of romance is communication.

ROMANTIC RESOURCES

63   How about a free subscription to the
      LoveLetter — "The newsletter of romantic
      ideas"?! Send your name and address to:
      LoveLetter, P.O. Box 226, Weymouth, MA
      02188.

64 How about an elegant, custom-made greeting card for your honey? Your favorite verse or quote will be rendered in calligraphy, and then decorated with a hand-painted flower. Around $50. Call 508-234-6843.

Passive people never live passionate lives.

65 Jim Rickert, "The Songsmith" will write and record original love songs for you! Customized with your names; available in any style (rock, country, ballad, etc.); and recorded on cassette tape! Call Jim at 617-471-8800.

CELEBRATE!

66 Celebrate your partner's "Half-Birthday" (the date exactly six months from his or her actual birthday).

67 Be prepared with a library of romantic music. Include: George Winston's *Autumn*, Natalie Cole's *Unforgettable*, Earl Klugh's *Heartstrings*, Enya's *Shepherd Moon*.

68 Buy her a wedding cake instead of a birthday cake!

69 Have a pair of elegant wine goblets etched with your names or initials.

Celebrate your similarities.
Honor your differences.

BE MY VALENTINE

70   You can get your Valentine card specially post marked from Loveland, Colorado! Just put your card and stamped envelope, addressed to your love, inside another envelope addressed to: Postmaster, Loveland, Colorado 80537.

71   Buy two Valentine's cards. Send one now, and send the other one in August!

Celebrate Valentine's Day 365 days a year!

72   Give your lover 14 Valentine cards: one-a-day starting on February 1st.

ROMANTIC MISCELLANY

73   Wear a tuxedo home from work . . . just for the heck of it!

74   Buy her a lottery ticket. Attach a note: "You're one in a million!"

75   *Barefoot Ballet*, a romantic CD by John Klemmer.

76   Being romantic isn't hard work. If you put your heart and your creativity into it, I guarantee you'll have a blast!

Romantic gestures have no ulterior motive.
Their only purpose is to express love.

ROMANTIC POTPOURRI

77 Book a three-day weekend at a romantic bed &
    breakfast.

78 Celebrate your lover's birthday for a month!
    Send a-card-a-day for an entire month.

79 Go on a picnic . . . in your living room . . . at
    work . . . at midnight . . . on a Tuesday
    afternoon. . .

Turn the ordinary into the special.

80 A weekend without TV. A day without the
    kids. An evening without interruptions.

HELP FOR THE HOPELESS

81 Change something in your routine. Get up an
    hour early and enjoy a leisurely breakfast
    together. Quit work at noon!

82 Write a love letter to your partner. Mail it
    using a special "Love Stamp" from the Post
    Office.

83 Visit Love, Arizona; Bliss, New York;
    Valentine, Montana; Loving, Nebraska; or
    Loveland, Colorado.

Romance is a state of mind.

84   Buy one blue gift and three red ones...two small gifts and one big one...three $5 gifts and one $25 gift.

HOPE FOR THE HELPLESS

85   Get every recording ever made by his favorite musical group.

86   Get every book ever written by her favorite author.

Romance is the process . . . Love is the goal.

87   Create "theme gifts" based on his/her favorite music, color, cartoon, flower, TV show, snack food, season or hobby.

88   Propose a toast. Take a walk. Go for a ride. Sleep in late. Write a note. Pen a poem. Sing a song.

FOR SINGLES ONLY

89   Mail her a copy of your resume instead of a greeting card. Attach a note: "I'd like you to get to know me better."

90   How do you know when to "get serious?" When intimacy becomes more important than excitement.

Money can't buy you love . . . but it can buy you a little romance!

91 Visit the place where you first met; where you went on your first date; where you had your first kiss . . .

92 Create and fill-out an application for the "job" of "Boyfriend" or "Girlfriend."

FOR MARRIEDS ONLY

93 Renew your wedding vows. Create a private ceremony just for the two of you.

94 Go on a second honeymoon.

95 Visit the place where you got married.

96 Have your wedding vows rendered in beautiful calligraphy, frame them, and hang them on the living room wall.

Definition of marriage vows: "A declaration of inter-dependence."

P.S. I Love You

97   Greet him at the door with confetti.

98   Run a bubble bath for her.

99   More recommendations for your Romantic
      Music Library:

      Living Inside Your Love, the CD by George Benson
      Openings, the CD by William Ellwood
      Forever Friends, the CD by Justo Almario

100   Indulge her passions. Fulfill his fantasies.

      Love isn't love until it's acted upon.

101 Ways To Be Romantic

101   Talk from the heart. Listen more than you talk
      Take action on your feelings. Express your love
      creatively.

      ***Your shared experiences and joint memories
      weave a tapestry that combines your two lives
      into one.***

Index

Fred's HelpLine is open Monday through Friday from 9:00 a.m.- 6:00 p.m. (Central Time), and Saturday from 9:00 a.m.- 12:00 Noon.

Call (713) 22-CARAT or
visit our website at: www.diamondcuttersintl.com